HYPNO-CYBERNETICS

Helping Yourself to a Rich New Life

Sydney Petrie
and
Robert B. Stone

CONTENTS

Achieving Your Goals

About Robert B. Stone

Robert B. Stone was an internationally known author, teacher, and expert in achievement of the human potential. He was author and co-author of over 80 published books, most notably on self-help and powers of the mind, with sales in the millions. He lectured worldwide on human potential and was an instructor at the University of Hawaii on activating the powers of the mind. A MENSA member, he had a degree from the Massachusetts Institute of Technology and was elected to the New York Academy of Science. A Silva Method lecturer for 20 years and Ambassador-at-Large for the Silva Method for 10 years, he introduced the Silva Method in Japan, New Zealand, India, the Soviet Union, and Thailand. For more information on Robert B. Stone, his life, and works, please visit robertbstone.com.

Books by Robert B. Stone

These are available in e-book and/or paperback. See a current list at www.robertbstone.com.

- The Magic of Psychotronic Power
- The Power of Miracle Metaphysics
- You the Healer
- Life Without Limits
- José Silva: The Man Who Tapped the Secrets of the Human Mind
- The Silva Mind Control Method for Getting Help from the Other Side
- The Silva Mind Control Method for Business Managers
- Create a Genius
- Celestial 911
- Martinis & Whipped Cream
- The Complete Book of Life-Changing Affirmations
- How to Benefit from the Coming Alien Arrivals
- How to Gain Strength from Nature Sitting in Your Living Room
- The Secret Life of Your Cells
- Life's Twists: A Collection of 100 Short Stories

WHAT THIS BOOK WILL DO FOR YOU

The scene is a control center for a large aerospace manufacturing plant. A number of people are feeding punched cards into an electronic computer. This is called programming. The cards tell the computer what it is supposed to do by feeding information into its memory banks. Later, the computer guides a space probe to Venus, landing it at a precise spot and on schedule to the minute.

Suppose the wrong information is fed into the computer. Would it still be able to guide that space probe to Venus? Of course not. It probably wouldn't be able to tell you the correct time of day.

We all live with the automatic help of our personal computer. It runs our body. We do not have to give a conscious thought to breathing, beating our heart, or operating our other organs and glands. It records our experiences and produces the attitudes and emotions we have programmed it to respond to.

Sometimes this programming is wrong or obsolete. Result: unwanted behavior, unwanted conditions of health, unwanted habits, emotions, and circumstances.

Children have been taken out of an elementary school where they have been doing badly and put into an experimental university class under the guise that they were exceptionally good students. Immediately, their spelling improved, their math made significant forward strides and their whole academic proficiency improved immensely.

What happened?

The new experience of suddenly being a "good student" instead of "poor student" reprogrammed them. Their servomechanism, called the subconscious mind, accepted a "punched card" with the information on it: "I am a good student." It then caused the students to behave accordingly.

There is a revolutionary new way to reprogram yourself quickly, easily, safely. It is called Hypno-Cybernetics. It has helped thousands of people to reprogram themselves for a more gratifying life.

Once you learn the three-step method (one step is sitting comfortably in a chair—it's that simple), you take just a few seconds to make contact with your automatic mind, and another few seconds to hold a mental picture of the new programming you wish to initiate:

A glance at the table of contents shows you that this book gives you precise, new programming instructions for every aspect of attaining a great new life.

Have you been struggling with health problems that arise from the tensions and anxieties of today's world? Then "reset" yourself for tranquil confidence.

Have you had money problems that find you inundated with bills and seldom anything left over for the good things of life? Then reset your computer-like mind for money in amounts that you never dreamed possible—all yours to spend in any way you want with even more ready to pour in behind it.

Are you tired of taking orders and feel that it is about time for you to give them, time for you to get the girl or man you want, time for you to make a name for yourself? Then program yourself with Hypno-Cybernetics for power, popularity, and influence.

- Attract cash.

- Stop smoking.
- Be a spellbinder.
- Increase your sexuality.
- Play better golf.
- Up your I.Q.
- Sharpen your memory.
- Strengthen your confidence.
- Be a better salesman.
- Increase harmony with other people.
- Set high business goals and reach them.
- Ignite enthusiasm.
- Radiate super health.
- Boast boundless energy.

There are no limits to the human capability—and that means *your* capability.

You have a lid on *you*.

It is a self-imposed lid. You put the lid on yourself by accepting limitations. Hypno-Cybernetics takes the lid off *you*.

As you turn the next few pages, you begin to program yourself for new goals, a winning personality, new pleasures, new freedom, new prosperity, new power, and new fun out of life.

And that's exactly what you get, starting immediately.

The Authors

1 – HOW THE POWER OF HYPNO-CYBERNETICS CAN GIVE YOU A RICH NEW LIFE ALMOST IMMEDIATELY

Know this: Today can be the day that changes your life.

Before you are through with this chapter, you will see a richer way of living begin to stretch before you like an open, inviting road.

It is not a road for everybody. Some people are so discouraged they couldn't care less about tomorrow. But you have already proved yourself. You have the spark that it takes to start yourself on a fascinating adventure. You have this book in your hands. You are ready for bigger and better things--for money, friends, fun and adventure.

You are ready to feel better when you wake up in the morning, achieve more at your work during the day, enjoy yourself with fascinating people in the evening, and drop off to sleep like a baby at night-with a smile on your face.

How is all this possible?

You have heard that we use only a small fraction of our vital brain capacity. You have also heard our phenomenal brain being compared to a gigantic computer which, were it to be duplicated by man, might fill the large Times Square area in New York.

Well, put one and one together.

Correct. We can now tap this vast reservoir of our mind. We can vault ourselves to new heights of health, wealth, happiness, power and success.

We do this by borrowing a technique from the computer world. But we do not have to be computer mechanics or electronic geniuses to do it.

A six year old can learn to use Hypno-Cybernetics. If you can operate the buttons and dials on a washing machine or a television set, you can follow the simple push-button-like instructions that await you in the pages ahead. In fact, Hypno-Cybernetics is easier to work with than some household appliances we've seen.

Actually, Hypno-Cybernetics should be taught in the primary grades at school. But it isn't, at least not yet. It takes no special skill to learn. No willpower. No consuming drive. Not even what we call ambition.

It is so simple, so easy, so natural that it just happens. It happens just as easily as reading this page, or wondering what time it is, or thinking about the opposite sex.

The dramatic fact is that when it happens, you could read this page twice as fast and with less effort, you might know exactly what time it was the moment you wondered about it, and your spouse or date might telephone you as you were thinking about the opposite sex.

What Hypno-Cybernetics Is

Take a look at the word Hypno-Cybernetics. You see it is a combination of two words—the prefix for "hypnotism" and "cybernetics."

Hypnotism is the modern means we have to contact a large portion of our mind called the subconscious or automatic mind.

Cybernetics is the equally modern means we have to instruct or program any automated device.

So Hypno-Cybernetics is a modern means to contact our vast subconscious mind and program it to do our bidding.

How L.B. used Hypno-Cybernetics for business success

L.B. had what you might call marginal success in his dry cleaning business. He did meticulous work. But he felt tense and irritable most of the time. His customers could feel it. He lost them as fast as he made new ones. Sometimes faster. A week after he tried his hand at Hypno-Cybernetics, he was at ease, confident and good natured in his shop. His customers felt his high spirits and responded to his enthusiasm. Business improved steadily.

When we say that LB. "tried his hand," we mean just that. Doing Hypno-Cybernetics means sitting in a chair and doing something with your hands.

How to put the finger on your subconscious mind

How does a hand or finger movement contact the magnificent subconscious mind? Every motion of the body, whether voluntary or involuntary, stems from the mind. The authors have been working with a simple finger movement that has permitted thousands to establish communication with their subconscious minds as easily as eating apple pie. No long trance-like sessions that are often associated with hypnotism. You just sit down and do it.

Once you learn this, the world is yours. We have seen our clients become the people they have always wanted to be, almost overnight.

Let's get one thing clear right from the start. Hypno-Cybernetics is not some mystical, occult, magical concoction.

On the contrary, it is scientifically and medically sound. It is a no-nonsense method used by psychiatrists, psychologists, dentists, and physicians, as well as by homemakers, students, and business people. It is successful.

Remember this about Hypno-Cybernetics-

- It is not mysterious.
- It is not supernatural.
- It is not philosophical.
- It is not religious.
- It is not occult.

Quite the contrary—

- It is scientific.
- It is natural.
- It is comfortable.
- It is effortless.
- It is proven.

"What Makes You Think I Can Benefit from Hypno-Cybernetics?"

The authors of this book are paramedics. That is to say, they work under the auspices of physicians or psychiatrists where weight loss, cigarette smoking, fears and phobias, or other health factors are involved. They also work with or without this medical referral or direction where non-medical matters are involved, such as the desire to be a more successful salesman, more efficient housewife, or a better student.

With or without the health factor, it is important that the au-

9

thors get across to every person who tries it this point: Hypno-Cybernetics works.

When we hear that common question, "What makes you think it will work for me?" We answer, "It does not matter that *we* think so; but it is absolutely vital that *you* think so."

What Your Mind Can Do for You

Your mind is wonderful, the way it works.

Doctors find that patients who have confidence in them enjoy more rapid recoveries.

Also, a person with rose fever who walks into a room with a vase of plastic roses begins to manifest all of the sneezy symptoms that he expects.

A salesman who does not expect to make the sale, seldom does.

Belief and expectation are like the main "on," "off" buttons that need to be pushed first before you can program the mind properly to reach its goal.

Take the matter of health. We may not want to be a Bemarr MacFadden or a Paul Bragg or a Rex Ravelle. But we all want to be healthy, free of pains and aches, and radiating attractiveness and energy. To get there, we need to believe it is our right, just as they did.

We may not want to be a Napoleon, or a Churchill, or a Lincoln. But we all want to be uniquely ourselves—creative, productive, admired and possibly even remembered. As they did, we must believe it possible.

We may not want to be a William Randolph Hearst, an Andrew Carnegie, or a John D. Rockefeller. But we all want to have enough money to eat well, live well, pay our bills, and travel, with enough left-over for our old age and heirs. Know that it can be.

The mind does it all.

It makes you sick or it makes you well.

It makes you live a life of a tired "vegetable" or a life of vigor and vitality.

It can be programmed for unending money troubles or good fortune after good fortune.

And Hypno-Cybernetics is the way to program your mind for whatever you want out of life.

That kind of programming automatically works for your benefit — always and unceasingly.

Believe it.

Expect it.

Everybody's "Got it" for Happiness and Success

K.L. was trapped. He worked at a job in construction which he disliked intensely, but his family could not afford to miss one week's salary. He was frustrated, hostile and depressed. How could he ever get out of this work and into something he liked without bill collectors breathing down his neck! He blamed his family, his boss, the world.

Hypno-Cybernetics now enters his life. He programmed his subconscious mind in several steps as follows:

1. Everything's going to be O.K. Don't sweat it.

2. A little planning can lead to different work.

3. Act like a free man.

It worked.

No biochemist can tell you how. Maybe the automatic mind sends signals to the endocrine glands. Maybe the metabolism changes. Maybe the blood sugar rises. What does it matter ... ?

K.L began to feel less tormented. He knew that a change would come, so he was less tense. His personality improved. He really did feel like a free man. He was able to get along better with his co-workers, and his family enjoyed him more.

He started to visualize himself in a place of his own where he could work on television repair. Now he was ready to "try his hand" at Hypno-Cybernetics again. He sat down in his chair and, using his finger signals, programmed his automatic mind as follows:

1. I will learn more about color television.

2. I will find a shop I can rent.

3. I will find a partner to be the "outside man" representative.

Inside of three weeks, K.L. was on his way. He took a night course; located a low rental shop on a side street; advertised for a partner with capital enough to buy the necessary tools and equipment. (And perhaps he fixed your set.)

"Either you've 'got it' or you don't."

True or false?

False.

Everybody's "got it."

Everybody's got what it takes to have all the love, money, good health, power, happiness and success that they seek.

We just do not know where the right "button" is to push.

Occasionally, somebody stumbles on this "button." He starts programming his automatic mind without knowing it. To the rest of us, it looks as if he just gets the breaks as he climbs the organizational ladder, travels in the best circles, captivates people with his new alive-ness.

As he passes by and gives us a big "hello," we look at each other and say, "He's got it."

Physical Attractiveness Can Be Turned On and Off

Two sociologists recently reported in *Psychology Today* magazine that good-looking students were more likely to get good marks in school than their uglier peers. Ellen Berscheid and Elaine Walster pasted photographs of students on their individual records and asked teachers to evaluate their I.Q. Identical records earned higher evaluations when the photos were of boys or girls who had been previously judged attractive.

What is also interesting is that the children themselves, when asked to identify troublemakers versus teachers' pets, chose the least attractive photos for the ones who were most likely to disrupt the class, and vice versa.

What the report assumed was that bad looks can escalate disadvantaged circumstances. But perhaps the cart was before the horse.

There is increasing evidence that human attitudes and human emotions can affect not only the internal health of the body but also its external appearance.

People who think mean often look mean.

People who are torn by worry and anxiety show it.

People who are friendly, look friendly.

People who always see the good side of life, shine with a special light.

Criminologists know that there is a typical criminal appearance of habitual inmates. Now they have found that when plastic surgery is used to change that classic criminal look, the men behind those criminal "masks" no longer act the part. Their rate of returning to prison is sharply reduced.

And so the question is raised in the case of the beautiful children who are the teachers' pets, which comes first: being loving or those lovable looks?

The authors have seen, time and time again, where a client walks in thoroughly unattractive and walks out like a magazine ad model.

How one transformation was made

Now, let's get this straight. The transformation is not always 100% *directly* mental, but it is 100% *directly or indirectly* mental.

There was Jaquie L. She was just a plain brunette when she was in her teens and a golden blonde when she was married. She tried being a redhead after her first child but she did not seem to fit the part, for by now she was beginning to look down in the mouth because that's the way she felt. She had put on more than 30 pounds since her marriage. The boredom and drudgeries of married life were beginning to show on her.

With Hypno-Cybernetics she used the following programming of her subconscious or automatic mind:

1. The best part of life lies ahead of me.

2. I am proud of my shapely body.

3. I see myself slender and beautiful.

4. I enjoy only nourishing foods and find that modest portions satisfy me fully.

5. I look my best-naturally-as a brunette.

Jaquie responded quickly and effortlessly to her newly in-structed mind. She became vivacious, happy and exuberant. Her posture improved as she appreciated the attraction of her own shapely curves to others, and she walked with a new, confident stride.

She dropped 25 pounds in seven weeks, without ever feeling hungry. Her muscle tone, skin and body tissues responded to nutrients. She looked years younger and more alive. She no longer felt the need to take attention away from the rest of herself by dyeing her hair an outlandish color.

Well, you say, anybody can improve in looks if she loses weight and eats sensibly. But that's a mighty big "if." Not all of us can change our eating habits at will.

Willpower Is Not the Whole Answer

Willpower is great. But Hypno-Cybernetics is far greater.

You are at a party. You see the hot hors d'oeuvres being passed around. You spot "pigs in a blanket"-those tiny frankfurters in dough. ("Dough-fattening.") A tiny voice inside tells you of the consequences. ("Dough-fattening.") The tray is coming closer.

("Dough-fattening.") Oh, just one or two won't hurt me, you say. And you reach.

Now, watch your girlfriend to your left. You know "pigs in a blanket" are her favorite, too. But what you don't know is that she has learned and practiced Hypno-Cybernetics.

"Swedish meatballs-my favorite," she says gleefully as she spears one with a toothpick.

There wasn't one ounce of discipline needed. She hardly even saw the fattening "pigs in a blanket." She automatically preferred what was better for her to eat.

It's a very short journey to beauty and attractiveness, to being more truly yourself.

And it's easy—downhill all the way!

To Live a Longer Life— and Fuller of Satisfaction

Some scientists, who understand the working of the automatic mind, now believe that it may be responsible for man's life span of some scant 70 years. In reality we could live much longer, they believe, but we are programmed to die around that age.

A Columbia University award-winning physicist. Dr. Gerald Fein- berg, began "The Prometheus Project" by writing a book with that title. He has now been joined by a number of other distinguished scientists, including Dr. Benjamin Schloss. Dr. Schloss deplores the fact that man is absorbed in changing his environment and seems to forget that he can change himself.

People dismiss the possibility of living indefinitely. Dr. Schloss points out, because they have been programmed to believe that evolution has given us 70 years and we're stuck with it. The Prometheus Project is aimed at re-programming us for a much longer life.

It is not as "far out" as it sounds. In his book. *How to Conquer Physical Death,* Friend Stuart asserts that the person who realizes *now* that he is immortal has conquered physical death.

Can you see yourself living on and on?

If you cannot, then there is no use hoping that anything like that will happen.

But when re-programming the mind c a n . . .

- Cure scores of diseases.
- Cause childbirth without pain.
- End allergies.
- Accelerate post-operative healing.
- Change aging skin pigmentation.
- Restore more normal sight and hearing.
- Diminish paralytic effects of disease.
- Stop unwanted bleeding.
- Heighten resistance to disease.

- Elevate total health.

… then one wonders where it needs to stop.

Hypno-Cybernetics will not teach you how to live forever.

But it will teach you how to add years to your life.

And dynamic life to your years.

How to Get Results for Yourself from Chapter 1 Now

Re-programming the automatic mind is not done with punched tape-like computers. It is done with mental images. Any mental image works, but Hypno-Cybernetic images work best. You can see for yourself how mental images produce what they picture. Try this: Sit comfortably, close your eyes, see yourself starting chapter 2. See yourself interested, absorbed, and convinced that here are the answers for your own life. See yourself putting the book down and doing each exercise called for.

LIME   ITEM   TALL   TEAM
TIME   CLIT   LITE   CITE
MILE   CLAM   MATE   LAME
MELT   EMIT   LATE   MALT
TILE
MAIL
TAIL

2 – HOW HYPNO-CYBERNETICS CAN HELP YOU ON THOSE DAYS WHEN EVERYTHING SEEMS TO GO WRONG

What to Expect in This Chapter

Now you start to work with the automatic mind. You see how it responds to your programming instantly and accurately to make every day better. You begin to see the possibilities that Hypno-Cybernetics has for you.

A team of research scientists at the Stanford Research Institute in California has developed a mechanical substitute for the brain. It can perform only a small portion of its functions. In fact, it can only direct the movement of the legs and the arms. But there is a parallel in what is happening at this institute and the technique of H-C (Hypno-Cybernetics).

So far, this Programmed Brain Stimulator has been used only for monkeys, but its inventors hope that eventually it may help persons paralyzed by strokes to regain the use of their limbs.

Here is how it came about. The researchers located 200 points in the brain stem of a monkey which, when electrically stimulated, caused movements in the wrists, elbows and shoulders for the arms and in the knees and hips for the legs. Then, they programmed a computer to send electrical currents in proper sequence for partially paralyzed monkeys to perform certain basic activities.

One sequence enabled a monkey to extend its arm, grasp food and bring it back to its mouth. Another sequence allowed the animal to scratch its back. Still another permitted the extension of the arm for the purpose of climbing. And there were more.

When placed in front of a set of buttons which were the switches for the computer, the monkeys learned which button activated them to perform the desired motion. Each was then able to touch a button and direct his own movements--reach, eat, scratch, climb, etc.

Of course, the analogy is a limited one. H-C uses no outside computer. It does not "wire us for sound." The buttons we push are imaginary buttons.

Also, H-C can help us perform an infinite number of "sequences," not just the basic kind used to help the monkeys.

Nevertheless, it is enlightening to know that the mind does in fact exist as an automatable electronic device and that it can be programmed. Writing in the medical journal *Stroke,* Dr. Lawrence R. Pinneo, team leader at the Stanford Research Institute, foresees the programmed stimulator as eventually used to correct behavioral disorders.

Research in the brain and how it works is being conducted on many fronts. Biologists have discovered that one single human brain cell may be "wired" to as many as 60,000 other cells. They have also found that when brain cells of mice are separated and placed in a solution, they proceed to join up and form connections; even insulating these connections to prevent "interference."

Is it possible to imagine the potential intelligence in the human brain complex of billions of sophisticated cells? It literally boggles the mind.

Let's Go for the Small Prizes First

A businessman asked the authors, "Can I improve my own business effectiveness with H-C?" When asked precisely what he wanted to accomplish, he rattled off a dozen accomplishments like "make accurate forecasts, accelerate growth, gain company recognition, make sound decisions, spur teamwork, develop long-range plans...."

We stopped him abruptly with a quick, "Of course, but...."

"But, what?"

"But you have to walk before you can run."

We had to convince him that matters closer to home, and closer to him, had to come first--matters like: get up on the right side of the bed in the morning, know how to end a headache or a backache or other nagging pain, look better, be more phlegmatic, end tension, master habits, recharge strength, be a real "good guy" at home and among friends.

It may take a few days, but first things first. Business is built on people and business can be no stronger or more successful than the people behind it.

The secret of "strong people" lies in the power of their own self-reliance.

They control suspicion, envy, and hate because they rely on their own statesmanship to rise above such negative emotions.

They overcome personality hang-ups and are able to "do their thing" because they rely on their own individuality.

They enjoy peace of mind because they rely on their ability to insulate themselves from strength-sapping circumstances.

These are the people with low doctors' bills, high income, and plenty of fun out of life. They don't even have a bad taste in their mouth in the morning. They are free of depression, grumpiness, and the kind of pesky things that "bug" most of us.

Self-reliance is their key to deal successfully with their problems.

Program yourself for self-reliance and you become a different person.

Are you ready?

Let's do it right now as follows.

Three Steps That Improve the Climate for Your Access

Read these instructions until we tell you to put the book down. Then review them if you need to, put the book aside and begin.

First, hold your arms out parallel in front of you with palms facing each other a few inches apart, thumbs up. Now close your eyes. Visualize a shopping bag over your left wrist. It is full of canned goods and is very heavy. Also, visualize over the other wrist a balloon filled with helium. It is so light it pulls your right arm up. Don't end this visualizing exercise until you can picture and "feel" the heavy shopping bag pulling down on your left wrist and the light balloon pulling up on your right wrist. When you are sure you have visualized as if it were true, open your eyes.

Right now, put the book down and do it.

If you visualized "as if it were true," that is, if you pretended the bag and balloon were really there, when you opened your eyes, you found that your left arm was lower than your right arm.

For some, it may be only a slight difference. For others, the left arm may have been slanted down sharply toward the floor and the right arm raised at an angle toward the ceiling, leaving perhaps a vertical foot or more between the palms.

Now, even if your palms were only an inch or less apart verti-cally, you demonstrated that you have the power to visualize as if it were true.

This is good. It is vital to your being effective at programming your automatic mind. Remember, we said that this kind of programming is not done with punched cards like those used for electronic computers, but with mental images, like those you just used.

If you are not satisfied with the movement of your arms in this exercise, practice it again. Do it until you see good results. Don't let your conscious mind move your arms. That is, don't move them consciously. Use your conscious mind to imagine the shopping bag and balloon. Forget your arms. Let your automatic mind do the rest.

What is really happening here? We imagine something and our body behaves as if it were true.

Suppose you visualized yourself inside a walk-in refrigeration room at a butcher shop. Would you start to shiver? Or suppose you imagined yourself in the middle of a hot, dry desert under the scorching noon-day sun. Would you perspire?

Chances are few people can visualize that realistically. But add the H-C factor and watch the difference.

A person using H-C will respond to the images of hot and cold in-stantly, because these images are reaching the automatic mind, just like punched cards fed into a computer.

In the next chapter, you will learn how to add the H-C factor to your visualizing. Meanwhile, though, if your hands move in the shopping bag test, you can move ahead on the way to attaining more self-reliance.

How to Clear Your Mental Channels So Your

Message Can Get Through for Results

Mrs. R.P. wanted to lose weight. She was using H-C to reprogram her eating habits. Three weeks had passed and everything was going along fine, except for one thing: she wasn't losing any weight. In discussing what might be the problem, she blurted out, "I guess I just can't see myself thin."

With that, the H-C practitioner went into his private office where he kept "before" and "after" photographs. He took her "before" picture and with some white opaquing ink he removed some of her outline in the picture, making her look slender. Then he returned and handed it to her.

She looked at it for a moment. Then tears started to roll down her cheeks. It was a psychological breakthrough. She was seeing herself thin, probably for the first time in a long while. From then on, H-C worked. Where she had been blocking it before, the mental image could now be formed and get through to its destination.

The next exercise is fun and quite rejuvenating. It helps to clear the mental path so the messages can get through. It is a relaxing exercise. Here is how it is done.

Sit comfortably in your chair with your hands on your lap. Visualize yourself in a gray room. It has four walls, a ceiling, and a floor--all light gray. The walls are impenetrable. Sounds cannot be heard. Even thoughts cannot enter the light gray room to run through your mind. You sit there in a mental vacuum.

No consciousness of your body.

No concern about the outside world.

No care about things you must do.

Just pure peace of mind for a minute or so.

Now put the book down. Get comfortable, and do it.

Do you feel more rested? At a higher level of well-being?

Our mind enjoys this rest. Even if it does not go one hundred percent smoothly on the first try, it is beneficial. And it paves the way for the final step toward self-reliance.

Final Step for a Brighter Today

Somebody once said that 99 percent of the things we worry about never come to pass and the one percent that does is never as bad as we expected.

As someone else put it, "Don't tell me that worry does not do any good. I know better. The things I worry about don't happen."

Worry is a killer. It saps our strength, darkens our days, and does things to our body chemistry. It can bring on illnesses, such as stomach ulcers. If continuous, these illnesses can have fatal complications. Worry colors our life black.

The opposite of black is white, the opposite of darkness—light. All we need to do is program ourselves for illumination.

The final step takes advantage of the first two steps.

The first step has proved to us that if we pretend something is so in our imagination, our body reacts as if it were indeed so. The imagined picture comes true.

The second step has enabled us to quiet our mind for a minute or so. It's like holding the camera still. This helps us get a better mental picture.

Now we will quiet our mind and picture ourselves an illumined and self-reliant person.

Everybody is different. We all have had different experiences; we are physically different; and we have different personality strengths and weakness.

What depresses, disappoints, demoralizes or "bugs" you may not bother anyone else in your family.

Similarly, you would need a mental picture to bolster you different from your neighbor. The third step requires a positive mental picture. It takes place in a room bathed in beautiful white light-to dispel the gloom.

What takes place? This is where the differences occur. It must be an event that you understand to be the ultimate in recognition-- something familiar because you witnessed it. What good is it to see yourself backstage in a dressing room with a star on the door, if you do not know from your experience that such a symbol is reserved only for the elite in the acting world. Or what good is it to visualize yourself receiving the black belt award, if you do not know its importance in Karate.

Here is a list of events. All have one thing in common: recognition. Select one that you understand. One that makes your heart swell up with pride.

- You are being toasted at a ceremonial dinner in your honor.
- You are receiving an ovation after being named the man (or woman) of the year.
- You are being carried on the shoulders of your admirers after scoring the winning touchdown (or hitting the winning home- run).
- You have just won a beauty (or physical culture) contest.
- You have just been cited at a company meeting for sparking a new company record.
- You are standing before the honor guard as a four-star general pins the Distinguished Service Cross on you.
- You have your right hand raised. You are being sworn in as President of the U.S.
- You are making the valedictorian address at your graduation.

- You have a letter in your hand. It says that something you have written has just won you a Pulitzer Prize.
- You are taking your place on the throne. It is coronation day.
- You are embraced by the most attractive female (male) you can imagine, who expresses love for you.

Select the one that you find the easiest to visualize happening.

Now, this is serious business. Are you ready for a change in your life? Or would you prefer to stay in a rut and just feel sorry for yourself?

If you sincerely want today to be a better day and if you are really willing to accept a life of rewarding tomorrows, the switchover is only two minutes away.

Instructions: Sit comfortably in your chair. Picture the same room as you used in the previous exercise, only, this time there are no light gray walls. Instead, you are bathed in beams of brilliant light. You see the event you selected in the above list happening to you. Enjoy it for at least a minute. Longer if you like. See it happening as if it were true!

Any questions? If not, put the book down and do it now.

The First Day of the Rest of Your Life

Betty L. was a loner. She got to her typing job at 9:00 a.m., left at 5:00 p.m. Nobody bothered her in the typing pool-or at the drinking fountain or lunch counter. She realized it was a lonely life but she was a nobody, wasn't she? So she accepted it... until she was hospitalized with acute appendicitis. She took a liking to an attractive young intern with a kind bedside manner. He asked if he could call her when she recovered.

Now, back at the office, she had something to share with the other girls. Would he call? What would happen next. One of the girls knew about H-C and arranged an appointment for her at our office. Not wanting to muff the chance when her intern called, she agreed to try H-C. It turned out that she had only three days. But that's all she needed. She programmed herself for attractiveness, self-confidence and out-going-ness.

The intern said how much better she looked, out of the hospital. They dated frequently. It was the start of a much more interesting life for Betty L., both in the office and out.

When you did the shopping-bag exercise, your arms reacted immediately to the image you put in your mind.

It is the same with any image you put in your mind. The action begins immediately.

The self-reliance exercise you just completed has started something. Without even thinking about it, you are going to walk and talk like a more self-reliant person. Your automatic mind is going to move you that way.

The more often you repeat this exercise, the greater will be the difference that you will be able to notice in your own feeling and opinion of yourself, what is called your self-image.

At first, you may feel as if you are playing a game, just pretending. But that's also how you feel when you first try to ride a bicycle. You pretend you can ride it, so that you can become conditioned to be a bicycle rider. Pretty soon the pretending is no longer necessary. Look, Mom, no hands!

Changes are already taking place in you. For some, there may even be a rise of one or two points in the pulse, which will later subside. Others may feel a desire to stand straighter with shoulders back and stomach in. Or there may be a feeling of exhilaration, or expectation, or lightness.

Go to a full-length mirror. See if you can't detect some change.

Do you look like a more self-reliant person? How is your posture? Do you see any improvements you might make in your grooming? Hair, nails, face, hands, attire?

If you feel an impulse to stand straighter or walk more briskly or comb your hair, do it, don't fight it. The image you fed into your mental computer is now behaving you. Let it. Only good can come from illumination, self-reliance and an improved self-image.

Today can be the first day of a great new life!

The High Voltage Power You Can Attain with H-C

The exercise in this chapter gives you only an inkling of what H-C has to offer.

As you learn the techniques described in the next chapter, your mental images become more powerful. You actually deliver them to your automatic mind with more voltage. The changes you seek happen more dramatically.

You discover that you have special talents you never knew you had.

You find yourself in the right place at the right time, whether you're looking for a parking place, or a better job.

You are able to express yourself better. The ideas begin to flow.

You begin to "read" people. It's more than their body language. You seem to know how they feel, and how they will take to you.

Your senses of smell, taste, and touch improve, become more discriminating.

Incredible changes can take place in good fortune and circumstances.

Much of this we do not understand. All we can say about it is that it is the working of the fantastic human brain, harnessed for more complete and efficient use. There seems to be no end of good that it can provide for us when programmed positively.

Later this programming will be more focused.

Instead of giving your automatic mind general "for motherhood and against sin" types of instructions, you will soon be targeting in on specific goals, even a specific girl, or a specific amount of money, or a specific kind of car or house.

How to Overcome Negative Thinking

Recent newspaper reports picture Mrs. Edward M. Kennedy as living with the specter of assassination in her mind. She dreads 1976 as the year Senator Kennedy may run for the presidency and, like his brothers, be assassinated. Psychotherapy, she is quoted as stating, has made her feel "more independent, more self-assured."

But apparently, she still has that dread.

Specific fears almost always require specific attention. In using H-C for them, you are able to locate the cause. Then you are able to take the whole package—the event(s) that caused the problem and the problem itself—and store it in the basement of your mind where other "dead" memory files are stored. By taking it out of the "active" file this way, it no longer activates you.

There isn't an unwanted habit—as smoking or nail-biting—that you now have that you can't get rid of quickly and without willpower and discipline.

There isn't a new habit that you would like to have—as the habit of saving money or the habit of being on time—that you can't attain quickly and easily.

How to Get Results for Yourself from Chapter 2 Now

Do the three-step exercise that transforms dull days into bright ones: first, the shopping bag exercise; next, the mind quieting exercise; finally, the image-building exercise that promotes self-confidence and self-reliance.

The first two do not need to be repeated but repeat step three as many times as you have time for. Each time you do it, you reinforce the programming. You become a stronger, more success-oriented person day by day.

3 – YOUR FIRST STEPS IN HARNESSING THE POWER OF HYPNO-CYBERNETICS

The following is an actual case history of a woman referred by a medical doctor to Sidney Petrie, an author of this book.

"Doc, I just don't seem to have any energy to go through the day. Even making the beds exhausts me. Maybe I've got some disease. Maybe it's my heart or my liver...."

"Wait a minute, Mrs. Jensen. I've just explained that the tests and the complete examination you received show no organic problem. But this does not mean I can't help you."

With that, the doctor began to write on his prescription pad. He tore off the slip and handed it to her. She looked at it.

"Who is this Mr. Petrie?"

If the doctor then attempted to explain Hypno-Cybernetics or hypno-therapy, the author would probably have never seen Mrs. Jensen. Who wants to be told that their problem is "in their mind?" He merely said, "Trust me, Mrs. Jensen, call for an appointment and see him."

When Mrs. Jensen arrived, Mr. Petrie had already been briefed on her case history. Yet he invited her to describe her problem to him "from the beginning." She told of her chronic depletion, her rapid tiring in the kitchen. "Even vacuuming the living room, I have to stop and rest four or five times."

Mr. Petrie listened attentively; made a few notes at his desk. Then he turned to her. "Mrs. Jensen, I think you are suffering from 'sensory distortion.'"

She paled. "What's that?"

Mr. Petrie rose and went into another room. In a moment he returned. He had two familiar cans, one that had held frozen juice, another coffee. They now held something else.

"Mrs. Jensen, hold out your hands please, palms up. When I place these on your hands, tell me whether the small can or the big can is the heavier."

Without a moment's hesitation she said, "The small can is heavier, of course."

"Weigh them on that postage scale."

She did.

"Heavens. I was wrong. The big can is an ounce heavier."

"I'm going to place these aluminum plates on the palms of your hands so you can't tell the size of the cans by their feel. Now close your eyes and let's try again."

She closed her eyes. "The can in my right hand is heavier." She opened her eyes. This time she had it correct. It was the big can in her right hand.

She thought a minute.

"You mean to say, Mr. Petrie, that I would find my housework easier to do if I kept my eyes closed?"

He laughed. "No, Mrs. Jensen, that's not quite it. But you're not too far away. We do have to cut off a message that is reaching your mind and causing a certain physical reaction. Just the way your eyes telegraphed a lie to your mind regarding the weight of those cans, a similar distortion is being telegraphed to your mind about your housework. You know this is true. You know from past experience housework is not that tiring. That's why you have sought help. With Hypno-Cybernetics we can correct this. We can even create a shift in the opposite direction. We can make your housework seem absolutely effortless."

Now Mrs. Jensen understood more about the mind. She became a willing and even enthusiastic participant in three sessions, each devoted to one of three Hypno-Cybernetic steps.

And that's all there was to it. The effect was immediate. No drugs. No weeks of therapy sessions. It transformed her into the young, energetic woman she used to be.

It could have been even easier for her. Instead of office visits, she could have used this book, had it existed then.

The Three "Magic" Steps That Are Not Really Magic at All

Three simple steps that are "magic" in themselves:

You could say they were as important as the three "R's"-reading, 'riting, and 'rithmetic. Instead of years to learn, they take only minutes. Still, though they can spell the difference between failure and success, despondency and happiness, sickness and health, they are not yet taught in school. Perhaps one day they will be.

Here's how easy they are.

Step One. You relax comfortably in a chair.

Step Two. You await an automatic finger signal that your subconscious mind is ready for your instructions.

Step Three. You give your subconscious mind direct instructions, ordering the changes you want in your life.

The details of the steps

Take step one. Can anything be easier than relaxing comfortably in a chair? We do this when we address ourselves to the television set, to a meal, or to the evening newspaper. Nothing to it. Only this time, we are addressing our attention to ourselves. Some of us need to learn how to do this.

Step two takes instruction and practice. You may never have performed this precise step before. Like anything new, you must learn it. Hardly any of us has ever consciously communicated with the subconscious mind. Still it is easy. Easier than threading a needle or writing a check.

Step three is holding a thought in your mind for a few seconds. Can you top that one for simplicity? However, what thought? And just how do you hold it? Here again you need instruction. But the doing is as easy as enjoying a piece of apple pie and three times as fast.

Add these three steps together and you get Hypno-Cybernetics— a simple process of adjusting habit patterns. For instance:

- You can change a habit of waking up at night to urinate into a habit of sleeping through the night.

- You can change a habit of detesting paperwork into a habit of getting through it accurately without hardly knowing it was there.

- You can change a habit of being quiet, retiring and miserable at social gatherings into a habit of being the most interesting person there and having a great time every time.

- You can change a habit of being grumpy and a downer about everything into a habit of radiating good cheer and encouragement

- You can change a habit of letting the next man get the

jump on you into the habit of always being one step ahead of the next fellow.

- You can change a habit of having periodic headaches, backaches, or other painful misery that the doctors can't pinpoint into the habit of feeling great day in and day out.

- A woman can change a habit of being less than fully satisfied in sexual relations into a habit of attaining bliss, and a man can change a habit, new or old, of not being able to perform sexually into a habit of always being a potent sexual partner.

- You can change a habit of indulging in too much food or drink or cigarettes into a habit of getting twice as much enjoyment in moderation.

There is really no end of habits you can change.

How to Break the Force of Habit Holding You Back

"But I have no habits," said one young real estate salesman, whose wife had just used Hypno-Cybernetics successfully to improve her ability to concentrate while taking university courses. He had called for her at Mr. Petrie's office on her final visit and she was expressing her enthusiasm to him for its habit-breaking power.

"What time do you get up in the morning?" Mr. Petrie asked the habit-denier.

"7:00 a.m." he replied. "But that's not a habit because I don't wake up at that time on Sundays."

"What time *do* you wake up on Sundays?"

"9:00 a.m." He laughed at the obvious trap he had fallen into.

"We are all the product of our past experiences and environments," offered Mr. Petrie. "Everyone of us is as we are because we are conditioned to be that way. The only one who cannot be helped by the reconditioning that Hypno-Cybernetics makes possible and easy is the person who has all the money he wants, all the pleasure he wants, all the friends he wants, all the love he wants, all the influence he wants, all the youthfulness he wants, all the energy he wants, all the happiness he wants, and all the good health he wants. He's satisfied. He does not want to change these habits."

"You mean to say I'm 'in the habit of' making only so many sales per month?"

Mr. Petrie told him of the exterminator who in two weeks upped his batting average calling on inquirers from 50% sales to 90%, and the new car salesman who was going to lose his job because in three weeks he had barely broken the ice but who was up there with the best of them five weeks later.

"You're a good salesman, too," said the young man, "How about Tuesday at this same time?"

This couple has since moved into a beautiful new home and both are enthusiastic proponents of Hypno-Cybernetics.

When you realize how much of your life is made up of circumstances that you yourself have created, you understand the power of the subconscious mind. Just about everything in your life is of your own doing.

You are powerless to change your life only because you do not know how to reach your subconscious mind. Once you learn how to reach your subconscious mind, you are able to reprogram it to move you—not in the direction past habits want you to go—but in the direction your hopes and aspirations want you to go.

How to Accomplish H-C Step One in Ten Seconds

Step One. You relax comfortably in a chair.

Sounds easy.

It is, if you know how.

How many of us will sit in a chair and feel relaxed because there's a load off our feet? Or because we have a cigarette or a beer in our hand? Or because it's a cushioned and upholstered chair that we can sink into?

Yet our hands can still be shaking from an exasperating day's work. Or our feet can be hurting, or our belt or brassiere can be too tight. Our mind can be running over all the things we have to do tomorrow or the ways we should have handled today's doings.

Relaxing comfortably in a chair means to be comfortable in both body and mind.

Here are some tips.

Pick a straight-back chair. You are going to have to do some concentrating in Step Two and Step Three, and those big plush varieties lull you to sleep.

Use a chair without arms preferably. Your hands are going to be on your thighs for Steps Two and Three anyhow. Chair arms might be restricting.

Loosen all tight clothing. We often don't realize how really tight our clothing is. Take your shoes off. Undo, unsnap, unzip.

Take a deep breath and let it out slowly. Feel your whole body letting go like a limp balloon as you let the air out.

Close your eyes. The moment you close your eyes you know you have shut the outside world from your thoughts and you are ready to begin Step Two.

All of this need take only ten seconds, once you have the chair selected. You loosen your clothing on your way over to sit down. You kick off your shoes. Take a deep breath. Exhale slowly. Close your eyes. And you are on your way.

Step Two—the Automatic Finger Signal

Step Two is a different story. It is something you have never done before. So you will have to refer to the text a couple of times in the process of learning the procedure. But you can learn this procedure in the next ten minutes by doing it once or twice with the book close by.

Why not clear the decks first? Do Step One. Assure yourself you have the right kind of a chair in the right room and that you can relax quickly and easily in the way described,

We'll wait....

Now for Step Two.

It is called the Automatic Finger Signal. It is your way of determining when your subconscious mind is ready to accept your new instructions.

Your hands are resting on your thighs palms down. You are very aware of your hands. You feel their weight on your thighs and you feel their warmth. Concentrate on this weight. Become as sensitive as possible to a weight difference. Does one hand feel lighter than the other? One hand *will* feel lighter than the other if you are keenly aware of the slightest difference in sensation.

As soon as one hand feels lighter, concentrate on the lightness of this hand, in fact on any feeling or sensation that comes into that hand. Can you feel the transfer of heat from that hand to your leg? Is the hand particularly sensitive to the texture of the clothing on which it is resting?

It is important that once a sensation of lightness is felt, you concentrate on this sensation. The same with a feeling of warmth, or of texture. Sometimes one feels a tingling sensation. Whatever sensation you feel in the lighter hand, concentrate on that sensation.

Now we are going to focus that concentration even more. We are going to center it on one finger—the index finger next to the thumb. This index finger is now extremely light and in it we feel the other sensations—texture, warmth, tingling, whatever the light hand felt.

Now there is just one more step and then something is going to happen.

Think of your heavy hand as on one side of an old fashioned scale where, when one side goes down, the other side rises. Your heavy hand is causing the lighter hand to rise. You feel this inclination to rise in the light hand's index finger. You know that this finger will rise. In fact, you feel it pressing less and less on the leg.

This concentration will actually produce a nerve impulse movement of the finger. It will slowly lift from the leg.

It may take a few seconds for the finger to lift or it may take a number of minutes. But lift it will.

This initial movement of the finger is a signal from your subconscious mind that it is ready to receive your Hypno-Cybernetic instructions. You give these instructions to your subconscious mind in Step Three. But you cannot do Step Three until you have successfully accomplished Step One and Step Two.

Try this now. Put the book down. Relax in your chair. Concentrate on the light hand, on the index finger, on its rising.

Most people get a very definite rise of the index finger on the first try. Some get just a slight or almost imperceptible rise.

Everybody gets a better rise the second time. This means greater contact with the subconscious mind.

Still greater contact can be obtained if, after you have received a good signal from one finger, you expand the lightness sensation to the other fingers of the lighter hand. You can get other fingers to rise, too.

In fact, you can concentrate on the palm of the hand, on the wrist, and on the entire arm and the whole arm will levitate. This is your subconscious mind activating the nerves that raise the arm. It proves that your subconscious mind is in close touch with your conscious mind. This is what you want to happen.

The greater the lifting response, the deeper is your Hypno-Cybernetic state and the more effective your "new life" instructions will be. Even a slight movement of the index finger is enough to begin Step Three. If the entire arm lifts, so much the better. But at any rate you are ready to start Step Three now.

Step Three—Mining for Gold

The subconscious mind is a powerhouse, a genie, a gold mine—all in one. And it is even more.

Scientists are still not sure how it works. A waiter in a restaurant admires a house, stares at it longingly to and from work. One day an old lady finds him in the restaurant and offers to sell him the house at a ridiculously low price that he can afford. And there he is living in the house.

The forces of accumulated self-images

The images that we hold in our conscious mind long enough to etch into our subconscious mind come to fruition. The amazing part is how other people respond to help our own mental images to materialize. Does one subconscious mind contact another subconscious mind? Someday, perhaps, we will know.

But meanwhile, this we know for sure: The better the hypnotic contact we have with our subconscious mind, the more quickly and more effectively the conscious imaging is etched into it.

We have established that contact in Step Two.

How to prompt the subconscious

Our subconscious is now ready to receive and act upon whatever we hold in our conscious mind. We can hold a statement in words. Or we can hold a visual image.

For example, if more money is your goal, you begin by saying to yourself the words, "I desire wealth and I will attain it." Or you can see yourself wealthy, that is, hold a mental image of yourself as a wealthy person.

The oral method is not aloud. You say and "feel" the words silently to yourself. The visual image is clear. You see yourself as you want to be.

Later, we will provide you with reinforcing mental suggestions or instructions which move you step by step to a more affluent, richer life.

Case history of a particularly aggravated problem

Sometimes problems exist that are much more perplexing, restricting, and serious than money problems. Take the case of Miss C. A secretary, 22, she was obsessed with the idea that she had what she considered to be a facial disfigurement. She felt this marring of her looks was upsetting her life. She avoided social contacts. She stayed home out of sight, except when she went to the office.

She did not want any help. She resisted all efforts to convince her that she had no such disfigurement. Indeed, she had none and was a rather normal, plain-looking girl. It was obvious to those in her family and at the office who knew of her obsession that she was really using this non-existing disfigurement to avoid social contacts.

She resisted all efforts to help her. She would not go to a psychologist or a psychiatrist. No type of therapy was acceptable to her. One friend at the office had even talked to a cosmetic surgeon about arranging an interview and possibly even going through the motions of a minor plastic surgery, but she said she "had no faith" in such an operation in her case.

She was finally convinced by her sister that Hypno-Cybernetics could help her live more comfortably with her "condition." She went to our consulting office with this goal in mind.

When she had finished telling her sad tale at the consultation, she was asked to move to a straight-back chair from the couch where she had been sitting and to relax comfortably with her hands palms down on her lap (Step One). Then she was led through the hand and finger concentration until first, her right hand index finger lifted, and a few minutes later her right arm floated slowly up until her wrist was level with her cheek (Step Two). Mr. Petrie suggested that it would be effortless for the hand to remain in this position for the next few minutes while she held a mental image in her mind.

"See yourself able to accept disappointments and the hard knocks of life without their affecting your peace of mind. See yourself willing to 'take a chance' in your daily life knowing that whatever happens you can maintain your self-confidence and serenity. See yourself radiating an inner beauty which eclipses any disfigurement. See yourself poised and in control of every circumstance." (Step Three).

She emerged from this session feeling that a load was removed from her shoulders. She promised to keep up the use of these mental instructions in her Hypno-Cybernetic sessions.

She became a joyful, more outgoing person and within a year was married to a young man who had one leg damaged in Vietnam. Perhaps there was a psychological link between her own imagined disfigurement and his very real one. *At any rate she had begun to live again.*

The Final Step Is Easier Than You Think

Step Three is easy. It is as easy as daydreaming. You enjoy a moment of seeing yourself as you want to be.

What do these life goals conjure up on your mind's eye?

"I am a great person."

"I conquer circumstances."

"I have supreme confidence in myself."

"I can achieve my goals."

"I think big."

Can you see yourself "great"? Can you visualize yourself the master of your own ship, able to ride out a storm, and go on to reach the port you started out for? Can you hold a mental picture in your imagination of yourself standing erect with a posture of confidence and just radiating success?

One young man told Mr. Stone he "just couldn't" see himself becoming what he wanted to be—a writer. "Publishers don't talk to amateurs like me," he said. "You have to be a 'name.'"

"Every successful writer was once an unknown."

"Yes," he replied wistfully, "but they must have had some 'entree.' They must have known somebody. Or maybe they had some 'inside' help."

"Inside help was exactly what they had. Their 'entree' was the words 'I can.' If you truly believe you can't, you won't. If you truly believe you can, you most certainly will."

This young man learned Hypno-Cybernetics quickly. He used one series of pictures in Step Three repeatedly: He saw himself a writer, sending off manuscripts, receiving checks, depositing them, then going back to his desk to write again.

In less than a year, these mental pictures came true. He sold his first article. It was about the power of the mind.

The Secret of the Mental Picturization

How does it work? Is it some kind of magic? Occultism? Mysticism? Of course, not. It is just plain common sense, applied in a very practical way.

Everything created in this civilized world started with a mental image. If it was a building or a home, that mental image became a sketch, then a design, then blueprints and specifications, then it was built.

If somebody saw that there was a need for a more comfortable bed and that possibly liquid instead of solid material could provide this extra comfort, that idea or image was then tried out in a small model and finally, the full size waterbed was born.

"I want to study physics."

"I am going for my master's in psychology."

"I just got my real estate license."

These everyday happenings were all at one time mental images. They were held long enough and enthusiastically enough so that they became motivating forces in the subconscious mind.

If a person really did not want to study physics but was just mouthing the words to make his physicist father happy, how far do you think he would get?

If a person really did not think he or she had the ability to become a psychologist but just liked to talk about it, would it be likely that a master's degree would be successfully attained?

And what about the real estate license? Does it not represent a true belief in the outcome, an acceptance by the person that he or she could and would become a licensed real estate agent?

These images, held "long and strong" enough, will move each person to make them come true.

Long enough might mean years.

Strong enough might mean a consuming desire that is always with you. You might think of nothing else.

With Hypno-Cybernetics, however, long enough means only a few minutes a session and maybe five or ten sessions in all.

And with Hypno-Cybernetics, strong enough means only that you can visualize clearly.

So you can accomplish quickly and easily the same life-shaping goals that others work long and hard at.

This is the magnificent ability of the subconscious mind.

All the Following Hypno-Cybernetic Commands Are Yours to Use Now

If you have gone through the paces of Step One and Step Two, you are ready, right now, to begin some "miraculous" changes in your life. For example:

Would you like to make six-hours' sleep as restful as ten-hours'? Then here is your Step Three:

> You visualize yourself sleeping for six hours. See the clock's hands turning slowly. See your body soaking up all the rest it needs. See your vital organs thoroughly rejuvenated. See every muscle, every tissue, every bone and every fiber in your body getting all the benefit from six-hours' sleep that it would get from ten-hours' sleep.
>
> See yourself awakening after-six hours' sleep thoroughly rested, full of energy and at a high level of well-being.

Would you like to get out of the doldrums and become a power-house of energy? Then here is your Step Three:

> See yourself changing gradually, as a flower might unfold in the sunshine. See yourself changing from "down" to "up." See yourself becoming more aware of the great pleasures and experiences that lie ahead for you. See yourself bursting with enthusiasm each day and overflowing with creative energy. See yourself enjoying your work as it carries you toward life's great rewards.

Would you like to become a more popular person, one to whom other people are drawn? Would you like to electrify your personality? Then here is your Step Three:

> See yourself able to *be* yourself. See yourself removing the "mask" that you have been wearing. See yourself getting out of the strait-jacket of conformity that has inhibited you from radiating your full self to others. See yourself now free to say and do those things that are uniquely *you*. To be spontaneous, original, and expressive.
>
> See yourself the center of attention and interest as others are attracted to your outgoing personality.

These are powerful commands. They program your subconscious to move you in the direction you need to go. The push is irrepressible. There is no effort needed to goad yourself on. No discipline. No spur. Indeed, it would take effort on your part to prevent yourself from becoming your new self.

These commands are particularly powerful because they are broad, comprehensive, general. They help you reach major long range goals.

In the chapters ahead you will find similarly broad commands to:

- Revitalize your health
- Add points to your I.Q.
- Make you a more effective executive
- Expand your influence over others
- Attract "lucky breaks"

However, you will also find more specific commands for accomplishing immediate results. These Hypno-Cybernetic commands will help you to:

- Cure insomnia
- Stop smoking
- Lose weight

- Become more attractive
- Overcome frigidity or impotence
- Heighten sexual pleasure
- Make more money
- Conquer any fear or phobia
- Improve memory
- Play better golf
- Learn any skill faster
- Increase physical stamina
- Get a quick promotion
- Find the right job
- Add to bowling scores
- See and hear better
- Be more aware
- Read others' body "language"
- Solve special problems
- Enhance intuition
- Be more creative
- Amplify extra-sensory perception

And accomplish scores of other major improvements in your life.

Conscious effort to break some habits and to improve one's life often fails in the long run. You may stop smoking, but then you begin to smoke again. When a diet ends, you often gain back all of the lost weight. Results from other "disciplined" changes can be just as temporal. Some changes are next to impossible through sheer conscious willpower.

With Hypno-Cybernetics changes are not only possible, they are always successful. They are easy. They are permanent.

You Can Create Commands to Achieve Your Unique Goal

You may have none of the problems or needs listed above. Yours is special. You may be the only person in the whole world with this particular problem or combination of problems. You may be the only person in the world with the goal that you have in mind.

Can Hypno-Cybernetics help you?

It certainly can.

In fact, it is designed for use by the individual to accomplish individual goals. You will see how scores of people have helped themselves with Hypno-Cybernetics, no one situation alike. This will help you design Hypno-Cybernetic commands just for you.

A retired person's dilemma

Mrs. G. is a retired school teacher. Her family has grown up and married. She has been divorced for several years. Now she frequently finds herself in states of depression, loneliness, and anxiety. She brings her complaint to her family doctor. He prescribes sedatives. She tries them and they help for awhile. But then she becomes dissatisfied with the effects of the medication. So she goes to a psychiatrist. Months pass and she becomes unhappy with a "lack of progress."

She heard about Hypno-Cybernetics through her son-in-law who has used it to stop smoking. She understands that the commands he used to break the nicotine habit are useless to her. But she realizes that if she could develop communications to her subconscious with Step One and Step Two, she could use this communication line to develop Step Three—the new commands she needs.

She gets good results in Step Two. Arm levitation in just a few minutes. She then commands her subconscious to produce to her conscious mind the reasons for her moody depressions. Then she sits in her straight-back chair with her arm in the air and waits...

As she sits there, she realizes that her present lifestyle is creating loneliness and anxiety. In order to end these depressions, she would have to go back into teaching or some other productive and satisfying activity.

She ends her session. Then she thinks about the critical appraisal she has just been party to. What should she do? What creative work is she capable of? She gets a number of ideas. Each time she rejects them. She is not able. She no longer can do this or do that.

A few days pass and she gets another idea. She gets back in the chair and the hand rises. She gives herself positive confidence-building commands. "I can achieve." "I have supreme confidence."

One month later, she becomes a partner in a new nursery school. She is today an active and successful business woman.

There is no end of benefits that Hypno-Cybernetics can bring to you. There is no limit to the success and happiness that can be yours. There are no bounds to the human potential.

But there must be a beginning.

That beginning is the three steps presented to you in this chapter. Take these three steps now.

Step One—the chair. Step Two—the "automatic" finger signal. What should you use for Step Three? Try this one on for size.

> I see myself learning Hypno-Cybernetics so that I become master of my destiny.

How to Get Results for Yourself from Chapter 3 Now

Do Step One, Step Two and Step Three. Give Step Two special

attention. The more of a "rise" you can get out of yourself the better. A movement of the right index finger is fine, but then try for all the fingers, then the wrist, then the whole arm.

Here are "instructions" for Step Three that will help improve your results.

> I see myself getting into a better and better state of subconscious communications each time I try. I see my whole arm levitating easily and quickly. I see my instructions being accepted by my subconscious mind and acted upon effectively.

4 – HOW TO SET UP A SUCCESS PATTERN FOR RICHER DAILY LIVING

What to Expect in This Chapter

Success—richer living—these are high-sounding words that seem like a castle skittering in the distance. The closer you try to get to it, the farther away it seems. This chapter brings that "mirage" right to your doorstep. You find out it is no mirage. It is real. You can walk into it and claim it. Everyday becomes a more successful day, starting with the day you are already in.

You have the key.

Hang on to it. Practice it. Use it.

The more you use it, the more successful you will be at it.

It is as if you were starting with a path to the automatic or subconscious mind, widening that path, then paving it, and eventually creating a veritable superhighway to your automatic mind for speedy and efficient communications.

Since your automatic mind is like a gold mine, a paved highway to it will certainly help you to mine it.

What better way to use it than to start today with programming that improves today, makes it a day of great satisfaction to you, a memorable day, a fine day, a day when everything goes right-a successful day.

The Many Faces of Success

In Chapter 2, we gave you a list of symbols for success because success can have different meanings for you, depending on where you are today and where you would like to be.

Albert Einstein said, "Try not to become a man of success but rather try to become a man of value." He provided this formula for success:

$A=X+Y+Z$, where A is success, X is work, Y is play, and Z is "keeping your mouth shut."

Ralph Waldo Emerson claimed that the successful man is the man who builds a better product than anybody else. "You will find a broad, hard-beaten road to his house, tho it be in the woods."

A third and rather different view of success is provided by Christopher Morley: "There is only one success—to spend your life in your own way."

There is certainly value in all three approaches to success and to the happiness that goes with it. Be capable. Be productive. Be yourself.

Most of us do not consider ourselves as capable. The "I can't" attitudes far outnumber the "I can."

Most of us do not consider ourselves to be as productive as we'd like to be. There is never enough time. Or something is always interfering, getting in the way.

Most of us never really get to be ourselves. We wear masks and play a part. We are who we want our family or our boss or friends to think we are. We hardly ever get to "do our own thing."

Just imagine what today would be like:

1. If you knew you could do anything you wanted to,

2. If you knew that there would be all the time you needed to do it, and

3. If, for once in your life, you could be yourself!

As different as the meanings for success might be that various people have, surely, if these three wishes came true today, it would be a singularly successful today.

And if everyday were equally successful, what a great new life would be ahead.

That singular day is yours for the taking.

The first day of a great new life is but an hour away.

How to Use H-C to Become More Mentally Alert

A blond, 30-year old Englishman can tell you the car and driver for every finishing position in every Indianapolis 500 race held. That's 55 races and over 1,800 car driver combinations. Donald Davidson knows just about everything there is to know about this annual event.

Ask him who came in 14th in 1935 and he'll tell you the name of the driver, the kind of car, and maybe how he was nearly eliminated in a pile-up just past the pits.

As a schoolboy in Salisbury, England, Davidson became passionately interested in this Indianapolis event. He would read all the news accounts and then send away to America for books on the subject of racing, and this race in particular.

Later, in 1964, he quit his job as a film projectionist and came to Indianapolis where his computer-like store of information confounded everyone in the racing business. It soon landed him the job as statistician for the United States Auto Club that sponsors the event, and a member of the radio team that covers the race.

Davidson is the first to admit he does not have a photographic memory. In other words, he cannot look at a fact sheet and then be able to "see" it at will and tell you what a certain figure is on a particular line. Neither does he attribute his skill to any memory system. The only thing that is left to account for his prowess is his intense "passionate" interest in the Indianapolis 500.

What is your Interest Quotient? (your dynamic I.Q.)

Interest causes us to be mentally alert. It opens our mental pores, so to speak, to everything that we see, hear, touch, taste, and smell.

We can remember the interesting things that happened in our life. But try to recall the details of some moment of boredom. The very fact that we remember interesting things means that they made a strong impression on our subconscious mind.

The formula is: greater interest equals heightened awareness, equals better programming.

The authors are now going to pique your interest in the art of H-C that you have just learned. By the time you complete this page and the next, you will be so thrilled with the possibilities that await you, H-C will be the most important thing in your life. You will want to use it for so many different reasons that you won't know which to try first.

In learning H-C, you have learned to do for yourself what hypnotists have been able to do for their subjects. You are now, in effect, a self-hypnotist. Anything they can do, you can do-and maybe better.

Hypnotism has come of age. Doctors, dentists, psychiatrists, psychologists and specially-trained people known as hypnologists use hypnotism for many purposes connected with health of mind and body.

The Uses for Hypnotism

Take a look at this list of uses for hypnotism. It is also a list of uses for H-C. It is only a partial list, meant to excite you with the things you are now able to do for yourself. A word of caution first. Although these things can be done by you, it does not mean that you should try to do them. Many are in the domain of your doctor. Look at this—hypnotism (and H-C) are being used repeatedly to:

- Provide relief for insomnia.
- Enable surgeons to operate without administering anesthesia.
- Add up to 50 pins to bowling scores.
- Stop itching skin.
- Halt nail-biting, bed-wetting, and other anti-social habits.
- End stuttering, stammering, and other speech defects.
- Induce rapid learning to speak foreign languages, to play musical instruments.
- Create time distortion between and during labor pains, easing the birth process.
- Knock 20 strokes off golfing scores.
- Concentrate hours of practice in any sport into just a few minutes.
- Turn jittery nerves into nerves of steel.
- Transform fear into fearlessness.
- End alcoholism and drug addiction.
- Switch food likes and dislikes toward healthy eating habits.
- Stop tics and uncontrollable spasms, including hiccups.
- Enhance concentration and learning ability, making average students superior students.
- Relieve migraine headaches, constipation, and so forth.

- Change wallflower and milquetoast types into popularity contest winners.
- Help job-holders to become business tycoons.
- Remember your entire life, as far back as you like, even to the prenatal period and beyond.
- Make the deaf hear and the blind see when no organic difficulties are apparent.
- Transform attitudes from the kind that impede to the kind that propel.
- End the smoking habit once and for all.
- Ease post-operative discomfort.
- Turn reluctant public speakers into dynamic orators.
- Change bad luck into happy circumstances,
- Help retarded children to learn simple tasks.
- Cure asthma and scores of chronic ailments.
- Stop fear of water, high places, flying, closed spaces, stairways, and the like.
- Heighten sexual pleasure for both male and female.
- Change habitual losers into winners in the business or social world.
- Turn off bad smells, loud noises or other temporary intrusions of the environment.
- End chronic heartburn or other gastro-intestinal disorders.
- Become more skilled with a typewriter, acetylene torch or other mechanical devices.
- Turn guilt, worry, anxiety or tension into blissful peace of mind.
- End back trouble caused by emotional problems.
- Reduce frequency and severity of common colds.
- Increase the sexual attraction you have.

- Heighten personal popularity.
- Solve a particular business or family problem.
- Magnify personal creativity and ingenuity.

Can you get excited about being able to rub your Aladdin's lamp and get any of these changes? *You should feel butterflies in your stomach right now!*

We know you are probably stunned by the wide variety of transformations that can take place using hypnotism or H-C. But can you see what they all have in common?

Of course—the answer is the human mind.

American astronauts are being taught how to program the automatic mind. To them it is just another computer. They may eventually use H-C to lower their metabolism on long space trips so as to use up fewer consumables. They may also use H-C to create time distortion and make long days of space travel seem like short hours. And they may use H-C to ease the discomfort of tight quarters, and give them the illusion of being more spacious.

While these words are fresh in your mind and while you feel a tingle of excitement, do three H-C exercises to build a success pattern for richer daily living. We will tell you how.

Remember we have established three requirements for this success pattern:

1. Know that you can do anything you want to.

2. Know that you have all the time you need to do anything you want to.

3. Know that, at last, you can be yourself.

End the I CAN'T Days- Begin the I CAN Days

"I can do anything I want to."

These words, when fed into your automatic mind, begin a change in you of such magnitude that if you did not feel the warmth and glow of it, you just would not believe it.

Actually, inside your mind, it is a very simple change.

You have been programmed ever since childhood to think that you can't do this and you can't do that. Parents have said "don't" to you more times than you can count. Teachers have put you down. Friends have scoffed. Flops—physical or otherwise—have etched their lessons into your mind "I can't, I can't, I can't!"

The simple change that will now take place is: the "I can't" programming will be replaced by "I can."

You really can, you know. Everybody's "got it."

There was a time when you yourself replaced the "I can't walk" programming induced by flops with the "I can walk" induced by helping hands.

As you grew up, you probably replaced "I can't swim" with "I can swim" or "I can't drive a car" with "I can drive a car."

Some of us never get much farther than that. But others of us who are more adventuresome change a whole raft of "I can'ts" into "I cans" by sheer demonstration.

Mr. Stone has taught creative writing classes sponsored by public school programs of continuing education for adults. They were less classes in grammar or English than they were classes in self-confidence.

"I'm not a writer," "I can't be published," "I don't have the time to write," were all changed into "I am" and "I can."

The results were that the students began to write and those who went all the way got published.

Get ready to put the book down; go to your comfortable H-C chair, if you are not already in it; quiet your mind and body; get a finger, hand or arm rise; and give yourself the instructions:

"I can do anything I want to."

Use those words. But also see yourself doing one or two things that you have always wanted to do but never thought you could. Picture yourself actually doing the "impossible." Keep re-affirming, as you see yourself doing what is now the "possible," "I can do anything I want to. I am confident and capable."

Ready? Great! Put the book down and begin.

There Is All the Time You Need and Then Some

A British writer recently said, with tongue in cheek, "Something takes as long to do as there is time available to do it." He was referring, of course, to the human tendency to slow down when there is no immediate urgency and to speed up when that urgency appears.

Did you ever sit down at a lunch counter in the middle of the afternoon? You may be the only one there, yet it takes forever until a waitress gets around to taking your order and even longer for the food to arrive.

Yet, go into that same place at high noon when it's so busy, you're lucky to find a seat. The waitress pushes you for your order before you've had a chance to see the menu and it comes out so fast you think the chef must have had ESP.

When people are geared for a high level of activity, they can get anything done, that needs to be done, in the allotted time. On the other hand, with an hour to dinner, you may not have time to get the table set for two.

Time is elastic.

If the automatic mind is told to replay in ten minutes a two-hour movie you once saw, it can and will. You could have seen it twenty years ago; it would not make any difference. And if you wanted that playback to take only two minutes, no problem—you'll receive it.

You are constantly experiencing the elastic nature of time. When you are doing something you like, time flies. When you are bored, time crawls.

You may be driving home in your car and get lost in thought. Suddenly, you're there. Your automatic mind took care of the driving and time became condensed.

Most people tense up about time. Maybe you are one. The very thought "I'll be late" or "I won't finish on time" makes it so. The tension interferes. It slows you down.

Also, by picturing or affirming yourself late, you are programming yourself to *be* late.

The opposite is also true. Picture or affirm that you get done everything that has to be done in plenty of time, you are programming yourself to be relaxed and on time.

The case of Miss R.M.'s frustrations continuously following her

Miss R.M. had difficulty in doing everything she was required to do at college. She was 36, had been divorced, and now was seeking additional training in the field of interior decorating. She liked this work and felt she could support herself at it. But she had a few things working against her.

First, she felt she was not successful in life because her marriage had not worked out. Second, having been out of school all these years, she felt nervous about being able to handle college work. And finally, she tensed up at every assignment, fearing that she would never be able to complete it on time. As a result, she tackled her college work fiercely like an overtrained fighter, and was unable to absorb anything. Even at home, when she followed a recipe, she was afraid she'd botch it, and usually did.

How can anybody succeed under those conditions? She had programmed herself for nervousness, tension and failure. The faithful servomechanism known as the subconscious mind was complying perfectly with these instructions. That's why she sought the help of H-C.

Once she learned the finger levitation method of contacting her subconscious mind, she gave herself two instructions:

1. I am able to relax at will. I feel naturally free of tension and at ease.

2. I concentrate at lectures and also when I read. No outside influences affect me. Whatever I concentrate on, I can later recall at will.

With the tension off, time seemed to expand. She had all the time she needed to do assignments. And they were handled more expertly because she was no longer in a knot. It all went so smoothly that in three weeks she had no more need to use these H-C instructions.

There *is* time to do what you would like to do today—with one exception: if you think there isn't.

The very thought tenses you up and makes itself come true.

How to Unlock the Door of Time

Are you ready to open up the prison door we call "time?" When you try the door you will find that it was never really locked at all. Time prisons are of our own making. Here is how to dissolve yours.

Get into a blissful state of deep repose. When you get a signal from your finger, hand, or arm, give your automatic mind the following instructions:

1. I do everything I desire to do confidently and with ease.

2. The more I do, the more I can do.

3. There is always time for what I need to do.

Look these three instructions over carefully. If you cannot commit them to memory quickly, write them on a piece of paper. Read the paper several times just before you relax, including the numbers 1, 2, and 3. Then, still holding the piece of paper in one hand, go into your finger levitation and merely instruct your mind as follows; "I accept 1, 2, and 3."

Clear? Put the book down and do it—now.

There Is Nobody Quite Like You in the Whole Wide World

"The mass of men lead lives of quiet desperation," wrote Henry Thoreau. Was he talking about their struggle for money? Or the problem of sex? No, he was talking about resignation. Men and women become resigned to their way of life.

Here is what follows that now famous line of Thoreau's: "What is called resignation is confirmed desperation ... a stereotyped but unconscious despair is concealed even under what are called the games and amusements of mankind."

Show us a person who has become resigned to a stereotyped way of life, and well show you a person who has a hard time getting out of bed in the morning. It does not matter if it is the 6:00 a.m. to 6:00 p.m. life that existed in Thoreau's day or the 9 to 5 day that most of us derive our "desperation" from today.

It is still a kind of psychological straitjacket that causes discomfort. Routine restricts, inhibits and smothers—that is, if we let it. And there's the rub—most of us let it. We let it chafe us and impede our freedom because we have conditioned ourselves to consider it an "either, or" situation.

When you were a child, you either had to stay home and do chores or else you could go out and play. Later in high school, you either did homework or else you did something you enjoyed.

It was either a question of work or fun right up until today.

You have just used H-C to program yourself to be able to do anything you want to.

How would you like to have fun at work? How would you like to be free of the feeling that you have to wear a stereotyped mask labeled "secretary" or "executive" and instead be free to be yourself?

This is the third step in this chapter's goal to make every day "a high day" when everything goes just the way you want it to and all seems right with the world.

Procedure: Get comfortable, get a levitation signal, and then give "yourself" these suggestions:

> I am confident in acceptance by others when I am my normal, unique, good-natured self.

> I am able to be my good-natured self at home, work, or play.

> By expressing myself, I unfold my highest self.

Ready, begin.

How to Get Results for Yourself from Chapter 4 Now

Tension and despair are killers. They erode our health and sap our vital forces. They ruin our todays and cut short our tomorrows. You can eliminate both, and any other similar obstacle to happiness, by this powerful triple play. Do H-C exercises three times. Be sure there is a period of at least a few minutes between each!

The first eliminates self-limitation and replaces it with self-confidence.

The second eliminates tension and replaces it with assurance and serenity.

And the third releases you from the prison of conformity and permits you to be yourself.

5 – HOW TO END YOUR MONEY PROBLEMS WITH HYPNO-CYBERNETICS

What to Expect in This Chapter

Money. Money is the short-range and long-range god of this chapter. Expect it to begin to flow at whatever rate you program yourself. There's plenty of it around. Claim your share.

You are a creature of circumstance. True or false?

Absolutely false.

You are the creator of circumstance.

You are able to invite unwanted circumstances and suffer their arrival. Or you are able to invite the kind of circumstances you really long for and live up a storm when they arrive.

They say the rich get richer and the poor get poorer. They have been saying that since Biblical days. And it's true.

The reason it's true is that the rich are programmed for wealth. They think productivity and abundance. They keep reinforcing their programming for abundance by counting their money. They think in terms of their assets and their income. They keep thinking how to increase those assets and how to increase that income.

The poor are programmed for poverty. 7
no money, debts and not enough income
their programming for being broke by d
at the bank, or their pile of bills, or thei
keep thinking of all the suffering that m

Knowing what you now know about ...
there any wonder that rich people are paving the way for eve
more money and poor people are going to lose what little they
have?

Somebody once theorized that thousands of centuries ago this
planet was peopled from outer space with the purpose of playing
a game called "limited love and limited money."

Who knows where this game originated, for a game it is.

There is no validity in poverty. This is a world of abundance.
Poverty is the poor man's choice—consciously or unconsciously.

You can use H-C to change your programming from want to
abundance. You can channel golden streams of wealth and glori-
ous new happiness into your life.

Money Games People Play

Money is a measure of product or service supplied.

In order to receive money, you have to be productive. That is, you
have to supply a product or a service. You can be a doctor or you
can be a service station attendant. Either way you are supplying
a service. You can be a diamond cutter or work on an automotive
assembly line. Either way you are supplying a product.

In order to gain in wealth, two things must happen. Productivity
must be pushed up, and costs of living held down.

A woman's lib advocate recently addressed a university sympo-
sium. She called attention to the disproportionately low numbers of women in managerial positions. She attributed this to

yths about women—myths that condition a woman
itations on her own expectations, to narrow her vision
world, and what she might do in it."

n she made her strongest point: "The really pernicious as-
ect of these myths is not that men believe them, but that
women do."

When we believe in limitations we are believing in a myth. It
turns out to be true, not because it was true all the time, but because our belief programmed us accordingly.

It follows that when we believe in our own capability to be productive and wealthy, we program ourselves to be just that.

People are constantly playing games connected with money.

The business tycoon often overeats, not because he has so much
money to pay for food, but because he subconsciously makes a
big stomach the symbol of "a big corporation" and affluence.

The woman who dresses gaudily can be exhibiting money frustration.

A man in Honolulu, who has been working in municipal sewers
for 25 years, eats his lunch in the sewer and when he is on vacation from sewer cleaning, he takes a side job for a private con-
tractor laying sewer lines.

And you've heard of the type who drives with car windows
closed in the middle of summer to make you think he has air
conditioning. Or the couple that runs out in wet bathing suits
in the middle of winter to make you think they have an indoor
pool. Legends perhaps, but nevertheless, indicative of the kind of
money games people play.

However, the most common game is the game of limited ability
to make the money you want. The pity is those who play it don't
realize it is a game. Like some football players who start swinging, they get carried away by an illusion and think it's the real

thing.

Abundance is the reality.

All we have to do is claim it.

How to Free Yourself of the Habit of Being Short of Cash

Mind control courses, under many names, are currently the "in" thing. They started in Texas, California, and New York and are now being given from coast to coast and in a score of foreign countries.

The main thrust of these courses is to operate consciously in the unconscious levels. Adults are being taught to examine the mental conditionings that now obstruct them. Of course, one of the major hang-ups is a feeling of limited self-worth.

If a person feels he is worthless, how can he or she develop a bulging wallet or bank account?

That negative conditioning or programming needs to be supplanted with a positive one.

Mr. S.C. was 56-years old. He was a very unhappy individual, never believing that he could do well at anything, make money or be respected. He had a lack of confidence and self-esteem. He had developed anxiety and tenseness. His attitude toward others was one of hostility and defiance.

Was Mr. S.C. affluent? Definitely not. How could such a man attract wealth?

He is now—because ...

Because he changed his programming with H-C. His new instructions were to think positively, to know he could do whatever he wanted to do, and to have faith in his business judgement. Whereas, he missed opportunities before because he was afraid to do what his mind told him to do, now he jumped in with confidence, accepted assignments, undertook new ventures. He calls H-C "the major reinforcement of my life." He is a relaxed, confident, and happy man.

You know you really don't need H-C to reprogram yourself. You can consciously think rich continuously over a period of time, and you will have acquired the habit of "abundance" thinking and the wealth will flow. It happens all the time.

Dick Jensen finally made it. The Sandwich Islands guitar player had a favorite daydream as a boy: by some sudden stroke of fortune, he would be booked to perform at the Copacabana nightclub in glittering New York. Fifteen years later his "impossible" dream came true.

But it happens quickly and effortlessly with H-C. No discipline. No remembering to catch yourself. No persistent daydreaming. No long period of erasing the old and substituting the new.

H-C gives you immediate access to that faithful computer of yours. The astronauts may do some of their own navigating but without their computers both in space and on the ground, they'd never make it.

Why don't you decide to "make it" right now? Start with cash. Then go on to bank accounts.

Here is how.

One of the great features of that mental computer of ours is its ability to utilize all of the previous information input in our combined experiences and translate it into a useful judgement in one particular area.

When you stop to think about that it is little short of miraculous. When you want to invest in a house, you consciously seek to recall what you have experienced in other house-buying or house-renting. experiences. But turn the job over to your subconscious, and the judgement is made on a thousand times that much information.

Turn the job over to your subconscious. That's the key. We have to learn how to get out of our own way.

Most people don't do that because they don't have enough trust in their automatic mental faculties.

This is really sad. They don't know what they're missing!

Are you ready to take a mental walk out of the world of the have nots and into the world of the haves? "Ready" means able to accept, as if it were true, a mental image of yourself as an entrepreneur, executive, or other post that involves money, responsibility, and the confidence to handle it.

"Ready" means a willingness to drop your present picture of yourself and concede that you have been wrong all this time. That is not easy to do. Nobody likes to give up a long-held belief. But the rewards are tremendous here and we hope you are not only ready but anxious to do this.

"Ready" means able to work up enthusiasm and, indeed, excitement over the new prospects that await you.

"Ready" means more than you have faith that changes will come. "Ready" means you *know* they are already on the way.

Get comfortable. Do your finger or hand levitation. When you get the signal that the wires are open to your subconscious mind, send these instructions:

> I see myself doing what makes me money. I see myself in the right places, with the right people, at the right time. I perform efficiently. I attract all the cash I need.

Ready? Go.

We want you to do this exercise again right now. But we feel that you can improve on the way that you just did it.

It's easy to say the words "I see myself." But unless somebody hits us with words like "sizzling steak," "dangling fish," or "glass of water," we do not usually go to the mental trouble of creating a mind picture.

This mental picturing is absolutely essential. It is what works the "magic."

Can you see yourself behind a big desk? Can you picture yourself a key man or a key woman carrying out important responsibilities? Can you see others coming to you to get opinions, authorizations, instructions, approvals, advice?

Can you see yourself in a brief mental movie doing a particular job in a way that you've admired others doing it?

Can you see yourself with a big wad of cash, paying a restaurant bill with a fifty or cashing a monthly paycheck well up in four figures, not counting the cents portion?

These are the mental pictures that you need to use right now. Create three situations before you begin. These are situations you can see yourself in. Memorize them—one, two, and three. Resolve not to go on to two until you see one as if it were real, etc.

Set up your three mental pictures. Relax and begin.

Blocks That Can Stand in the Way of Your Prosperity

When a country suffers an economic setback, we call it a depression. The gross national product—that is, the total amount of goods and services produced—shrinks. Business people retrench. They cut down on expenses, reduce labor overhead, and exhibit little confidence in the future.

It soon becomes more than a business depression. People who lose their jobs are depressed. The industrialists who see their curve of sales nosedive are depressed. Proprietors of small businesses have trouble paying the rent and get depressed. And their landlords get depressed. And how do you think the President of the country feels? And Congress?

A British psychiatrist recently reported in the *British Medical*

Journal that the amount of depression and suicide dropped sharply in Northern Ireland during 1971 and 1972, one of the bloodier periods of the civil war. Belfast, hardest hit by violence, showed the least incidence of mental depression. County Down, the most peaceful area, the most. Psychiatrists have long theorized—and this seems to bear it out—that depression results when aggressive impulses are thwarted or inhibited.

The Fruits of Frustration—How They're Forced on You

What is the connection with money? Mental depression and its partner in poverty, economic depression, derive largely from thwarted or inhibited economic aggression.

We want to enjoy good things. But we can't.

We want to pay our bills, but we can't.

She wants that dress. But she doesn't have the money. He wants that car. But no chance.

The frustration brings mental depression. Mental depression perpetuates economic depression.

How do we end mental depression so we can enjoy prosperity? Avoid the frustration.

Canceling frustration from the present picture is easy with H-C.

Let's call frustration "Block No. 1." After we list the chief blocks to having all the money we want, well go to work with the right block busters.

Remember the shopping bag experiment you did? You closed your eyes, visualized a heavy load on your extended left arm and a light balloon pulling up your right arm. You opened your eyes and found that your arms had responded to this visual image.

Well, not only our body responds to our mental images, but somehow other people respond to our mental images and, eventually, the world of circumstances we live in seems to respond to these mental images.

To those who have always thought they were *creatures* of circumstances, it may now come as a shock to realize you are instead the *creators* of circumstances.

How to Control Frustration

What we hold in our mind's eye creates circumstances.

Is there any wonder that the person who keeps thinking about his dark today and darker tomorrow seldom sees the sun?

Like the weather, everybody talks about positive thinking, but nobody does anything about it.

When you picture the problem in your mind, your body, everybody, the world around you, generates that problem.

So what do you do about it? Stop thinking? No. Start picturing the solution.

If you dwell on the problem, you are in there rooting for the problem, whether you want to or not.

If you would rather root for the other team, just dwell instead on the solution.

The poor get poorer because they hold poverty pictures in their self-pitying minds.

The rich get richer because they are always counting future profits in their self-gratifying minds. Can you imagine what would happen to the millionaire who kept imagining the worst?

And can you imagine what would happen to you if you kept imagining the best?

Put "negative imaging" down as Block No. 2.

Mr. L.R. was a moderately successful businessman, the president of his own small manufacturing company, and happily married to a charming wife. He was a rather unattractive, sloppily dressed, overweight man in his middle forties when he first came in for H-C assistance.

"I want to command more respect in my company," he explained.

"Whenever I talk to an employee, I keep getting the feeling he's thinking, 'You stupid fat slob, who are you to tell me what to do?' "

L.R. recognized that these feelings were not reality rooted. But for as long as *he* felt them, he was interfering with his own effectiveness and undermining his own authority. Production and profits were not what they should be.

Use of a regression technique

At first H-C did not work. Attempts to reinforce L.R.'s own self-esteem, based on his competence in building the company and directing its success, did not seem to get anywhere.

Then a regression technique was used. L.R. was asked to put himself into communication with his subconscious mind via the finger levitation method. He was then asked to visualize himself talking to one of his employees and experiencing the feeling that such put-down thoughts were being leveled at him.

Then he was asked to travel back in time to the first time that he could recall experiencing similar feelings. He did this and then began to recall a time when he was in his late teens, enthusiastically talking about getting a date with a particular girl. He remembered his father telling him that such a pretty and bright young girl could have her choice of any number of dates. So why should she choose to go out with him? L.R. remembered he began to cry as he felt put-down by his father whose approval he was constantly trying to win.

Now the problem was easy to solve. H-C mental pictures were

73

directed at reinforcing his knowledge that he was no longer a 17-year-old trying to get a date with a pretty girl, but that he was a man successfully married to a beautiful and charming wife whom he found very desirable and who he felt loved him as much as he loved her. He kept programming his automatic mind for a self-image of success at home and office.

A few such sessions and his self-worth rose high above such temporal matters as obesity and appearance, factors which could readily be changed. In a total of 27 H-C sessions over a period of a couple of months, the critical feeling at the office totally disappeared and was supplanted by one of competent authority.

Production rose. Profits increased. And as a side bonus, he lost 20 pounds and became style conscious.

Put your finger on self-worth as Block No. 3 to money in the bank.

As in the case of L.R., a block such as self-worth may be deeply rooted in some past experience. In a future chapter, we will elaborate on the "railroad" method of going back in time to re-member such experiences and attack them with specific H-C reprogramming.

Meanwhile, you may not need to do this. We will assume you can gain significantly by removing these blocks via the direct approach. Later, you can attack specific deep rooted causes if they appear to be delaying the cash flow.

Block Busters That Let Loose a Flood of Wealth

The three blocks to a free flow of money in your direction are therefore:

Block No. 1 —Frustration

Block No. 2—Negative Imaging

Block No. 3-Self-Worth

They are in your automatic mind. They need to be removed and replaced.

Doctors still do not know how hypnotic effects actually come about. They watch as a hypnotized person is made to see, feel, and do remarkable things. But they cannot explain what they see. They watch as the hypnotized man creates a numbness in his hand until it can feel no pain. They listen as he talks readily about the past and his troubles' origins. They examine as symptoms of illnesses disappear on command.

But they cannot explain it.

They can only use it successfully.

How to Use Your H-C to Blast Road Blocks

You are now about to use H-C successfully to make you rich. It is like taking away the old blueprint that your mental factory is using and substituting a new blueprint.

The new product is "more money."

Now for the new blueprint, or more exactly-new programming.

Warning: This is like TNT. It is literally explosive in its effect. It can put you in a deluge of wealth before you are ready for it.

Some may prefer to put the book down right now and wait for a day or so while they accustom themselves to a new kind of future.

If so, see you later.

If you are ready to proceed now, here is Blockbuster No. 1.

Put the book down, do your finger rise exercise, and visualize as follows:

> I accept my financial condition as it is today as a temporary condition. I have no anxiety about it, I see myself happy. I am confi-

dent about tomorrow.

Do it.

You can follow up in a few minutes with Blockbuster No. 2. Take a stretch. Get a cold drink.

As you drink the cold liquid, visualize yourself going from problem to solution.

Here is Blockbuster No. 2.

Put the book down, relax, do your finger levitation, and picture as follows:

> I no longer put creative energy into problems. Instead, I visualize solutions. I no longer think of the little money I have. Instead, I think of myself as prospering and rich. I plan for a wealthy future.

Do it. Just don't read about it.

The Final Blockbuster

In a few minutes you will be ready for the third Blockbuster. Take another stretch. Perhaps you'd like to finish that glass of water. As you swallow, think of yourself as gaining assets, instead of water, with every swallow you take.

Here is Blockbuster No. 3.

Put the book down, enter your blissful state of deep relaxation until you get the nod from your finger, then visualize:

> I am rich in experience, knowledge, talent, and capability. I see myself as the most valuable person I know. I see myself climbing the ladder of success to the top. That is where I know I belong.

Do it now.

An Instant Cash Bonus Builder

Want proof that something is at work for you right now?

We mean the kind of proof that you can spend now—green

money.

If you have a problem about money and need some extra cash, here is how to get it quickly.

Relax, get the finger movement, and then think with expectation:

> My needs are supplied. I see myself with more money to solve a money problem. I don't need to know where it comes from. I just see that it has come!

Do it now.

How to Get Results for Yourself from Chapter 5 Now

Stop thinking about the money problem. Start thinking about all money problems solved. Think about the solution.

Do the three Blockbuster H-C exercises. Pause between them and get ready for a change each time.

Accept a cash bonus right now by doing the final H-C exercise. Expect to have more money.

You won't have long to wait.

6 – HOW TO ACHIEVE POWER AND CONTROL OVER EVERYONE YOU MEET

What to Expect in This Chapter

The ability to attract people and to influence them to do your bidding is closer than you think. First you get close to them. Then you polish your magnet. Here's where your body is going to speak volumes for you, as you sit back confidently and watch the miracles happen

Early hypnotists believed in a magnetism through which one person could control another. They thought it similar to the power used by certain species of snakes who fix their eyes on a bird or other potential dinner. The bird appears to be fascinated. It loses its will or ability to fly away and flutters helplessly as the snake moves in for the kill.

In 1770, Frederick Anton Mesmer created a name for himself by using an invisible force he called "animal magnetism." He effected cures for thousands weekly in Vienna. Mesmerize still remains a byword for one person controlling another by some hypnotic force.

A much more powerful force is used in this chapter. It makes mesmerism seem like hit or miss child's play.

Still it is valuable to take a second look at Mesmer's magic and especially the magnetism of the serpent. For instance, suppose you were to put yourself in the position of the transfixed bird? What would you feel?

Probably you would feel an attractive force. Magnetism does not overwhelm by force. It attracts. You, as the bird, feel an unexplainable attraction to the snake. You have no desire to fly away. The fluttering of your wings indicates an excitement of the moment.

It is the excitement of attraction.

The Most Powerful Force in the World

Attraction is the most powerful force there is.

To attempt to compel a person by other forces such as physical force, by fear or by threat, sets up a natural resistance.

To attract a person by physical "body language," by admiration and respect, or by a high level of rapport must always be effective because there is no resistance.

When there is no resistance, you are able to achieve power and control. People are attracted to you like flies to molasses. And they stick.

We are going to turn on the force of attraction in the next few pages. However, there is one prerequisite. It is a mental matter, but quite important to tackle right now.

If you don't want to attract people, you will not be able to do an attraction H-C exercise effectively. Your underlying reticence will interfere. So you must want to attract people into your area of sexual influence, social influence or business influence so that your control can be exercised.

This underlying reticence to attract people has different aspects in everybody. But there is one common denominator: A feeling of separateness.

If you feel separate, you are reinforcing separateness, and undermining the force of attraction.

Here are some of the factors that often make us feel separated from other people:

- They speak differently.
- They wear different clothes.
- They have beards or unusual hair.
- They believe religiously differently from us.
- They don't drink liquor while we do, or vice versa.
- They are vegetarians or eat differently.
- They are paraplegics or handicapped.
- They have a life-style that is strange to us.
- They drive a freaky car or don't drive at all.
- They exhibit strange mannerisms.

Can you spot one thing common to these ten strange classes of people? Take another look. That's right: the word "they." They are all people.

We seldom think of that, though. We spot the differences. Then we dwell on the differences. Our body reflects our thoughts. It speaks "separation."

Watch what happens when we program ourselves for "togetherness," or a feeling of closeness.

The closeness is reflected in our body language. The other person picks it up and feels a closeness, too. That spells attraction.

When people are attracted to you, you control them. When they do not feel any attraction or rapport, your influence is nil.

Now, these don't have to be the people in the above ten categories. They were selected to illustrate the point, so they are exaggerated differences. A smaller difference that we may not even be aware of can give us the same feeling of separation if we let it.

The trick is to be programmed to notice the similarities not the differences.

The feeling of closeness that results gives you more power of people. You will be amazed how they literally follow you around and seek to do your bidding.

Here is your H-C command:

> I feel close to people. I have a genuine attitude of togetherness. I respect them for any differences. But I see all people in the family of Man.

This is an exhilarating exercise. It can do more for the doer than anybody else at this moment. But then the reprogrammed body will begin to spellbind others.

Put the book down now, relax, and visualize kinship with all mankind.

How to Make Your Body Speak Power and Attraction

Personal attraction can be based on striking physical attractiveness, as we all know. However, this type of attractiveness-be it of the male or female-compared to an inner magnetism, is simply not in the big league.

You can do things with your body that eclipse skin level attractiveness—things with your hands, legs, face, voice, stance, posture, and more.

Let's take a look at hands. We gesture, we explain, we indicate —all with hand movements. Did you ever watch a foreman at a construction site motioning directions to a lift operator? Not a word is spoken.

Or did you ever watch a taxi driver get mad at another driver his voice could no longer reach? His hands do the talking.

In Hawaii, they do the hula, a dance with swaying hips, but the lyrics are "sung" with the hands.

Be aware of hands. Watch what other people's hands are doing. Be aware of what your own hands are "saying."

> She just put her hand on your arm.

> He is drumming his fingers on the table.

> She is folding her hands on her lap.

> He is moving his hands in a fidgety manner.

What does it mean about him, about her, to you?

If you have a feeling of separateness concerning them, you probably couldn't care less. And they feel it. They feel a corresponding separateness from you.

But you have a feeling of rapport with them. You care. You respond to their mood as expressed by their body language. And they feel that, too. They feel attraction to you.

You are gaining a power over them.

How about learning some of the vocabulary of body language?

A woman is talking to a man. She stands at a "safe" distance. She's saying she is not interested.

Another woman is now talking to that same man. She moves really close. She is said to be invading his "territory." As she talks, she puts one hand on his arm or his chest. Perhaps there is an almost imperceptible stroking motion. She is saying in effect, "I'm yours." What a pity if he's not "listening."

A third woman is now talking to that same man. She not only invades his territory, but she is all over him. One arm is around him, another pets his shoulder. Her whole body is agitated. What is she saying? She is trying to say the same as woman number two but she is overdoing it, overreacting, and the alert male can see through it. She is either "buttering" him up or trying to throw a smoke screen around her own frigidity.

Have you ever seen somebody who looks as though he had no apparent interest in what you were saying? Here's one such person now. He looks at you only for a second then looks away with apparent disinterest. See the way he is now sprawled on the chair in an indifferent way. Now he gets up and stands with his hands slightly back of normal side position, as if he felt "challenged." What such a person is really saying is "I like you. I would like to work with you. But I don't want you to know it. You might reject me. And I cannot stand to be rejected."

Is he in your power? You bet he is—if you recognize it.

Do you detect a blush when you see it? It can be just a slight flush, barely visible. Both men and women blush. It means sexual arousal or any other kind of emotional arousal. You can control your own blush by controlling your emotions. (H-C exercise: "I see myself placid in the face of any emotional arousal. I play it cool.") You can be alerted to the avenues of control by other people's blushes.

Perspiring is a sign of fright. So is turning pale, or shortness of breath. A sweating person is exposing his anxiety. You take it from there. Will you feed and exploit that anxiety? If the answer is yes, you just lost your power over him, that is, unless you just want a temporary whip over him, like the racketeer. To exert real power, you don't feed the anxiety or fear, you express your understanding in a diplomatic way.

You show your kinship with him. He'll follow you anywhere.

What do we do about body language? How do we use it, benefit from it to make our influence and power felt?

First, we must learn to control our own body language.

Second, we must learn to read other people's body language.

Take the matter of self-control.

Mary Smith reviews this chapter. She sees one or two of these tendencies within her. She blushes easily. She begins to stutter when she gets excited. She analyzes the causes. She recognizes the problems. This mental process, alone, is a giant step toward eliminating these body games or symptoms.

What we are really doing in this critical analysis is understanding ourselves. This understanding leads to a harmony between our conscious feeling and our body. There is less of a need for the body, then, to assert itself—to play its game.

Then, without the symptom, we are free of a self-perpetuating condition. We gain new confidence. We express it to others.

Mary Smith then uses the following H-C exercise to reinforce her control. She throws in an extra programming instruction to become more aware of others' body language. It goes like this:

> I no longer need to express my private feelings and secret reactions by body language. I understand these feelings and I recognize them without body signs. 1 also recognize these signs in others. I know what they mean. They help me to feel understanding and empathy for others.

Remember the wild scene in NASA's Houston Mission Control when the safe lunar landing was made. The sound did not come from there as the commentator switched on only the video. So you viewed the exultation but could not hear it. Still, nothing was lost. The back slapping, hand shaking, and hugging told the whole relieved, happy story.

The silent language is often louder than the spoken. The H-C instructions you are about to give yourself inhibit only the body language you want to tone down. Later, you will give yourself instructions to reinforce what you want expressed.

Put down the book. Relax deeply. Get a good finger, hand or arm levitation and give yourself the above body language instruction for the control of yourself and others.

How to Program Yourself for Stature and Power

Napoleon was a short man. History provides many examples of

short men who became dictators. However, tall men are the ones whom we all look upon as born leaders. Is tallness strictly a physical quality? Can we appear to be taller than we are? Let's take a look at this.

Sigmund Freud, the father of psychoanalysis, discovered that when people feel differently about themselves and others, they change their behavior patterns. The man who stops seeing himself as a weakling who must be subservient to other men begins to be a much more manly person.

After Freud's time, another discovery was made: behave like the man or woman you want to be and you begin to feel as you behave.

It sounds like the tail wagging the dog. But stand up straight and you feel ready to lick the world. Slouch, and you feel licked by the world. Try it.

Walk "tall" and you feel like a proud leader.

Smile, as those smile buttons encourage you to, and you become a more friendly person.

Talk a bit louder, shake hands more firmly, and you feel yourself becoming a more forceful person.

We can control the power we have in our own eyes, as well as other people's eyes, by the way we behave.

The physical image of a powerful person now becomes doubly important.

You have arrived at a party. The people are strangers to you. You look around to spot somebody you find attractive. Are you attracted to the person over there who is drinking too much and talking too loud, as if to say, "Hey! Look at me."

Are you attracted to the milquetoast on the other side of the room who is all hunched up and trying to blend in the wallpaper?

How about the person sitting alone on the couch, looking around nervously and puffing at a cigarette furiously?

Probably not.

Now take a look over there. That person is sitting in a comfortable position. Notice the relaxed pleasant smile, hardly any body movement, no noticeable tension. That person has the situation well in hand and is worth meeting.

The self-confident look is easy to acquire. It is more a case of not doing certain things—avoiding nervousness and its mannerisms; not showing any tension or uncertainty, instead keeping the body loose, limp and relaxed; and it means keeping body movements to a minimum, maintaining an air of nonchalance and of focused attention.

The self-confident look is interpreted as superiority. We look up to such a person. It is so at a party. It is so at a business meeting.

The company directors and department heads are at a conference. Two junior execs are sounding off at each other, each trying to argue their points convincingly. The senior executives are sitting back in their chairs as though they've heard it all before. The table-pounding, rapid hand movements and raised voices don't seem to bother them as they move their heads back and forth from one to the other like solons.

Now, one of the senior executives is making a statement. All eyes are on him. You get the feeling that here is the answer. The issue is being decided. Why? Because this executive has set the stage. He has primed everybody through his body language. The actual virtues or merits of what he has to say are secondary.

Let's backtrack and watch his body language. He is sitting back in a relaxed position. He concentrates on the discussion with no side remarks to his colleagues. Slight tension lines around his eyes bespeak his concentration. Occasionally, his eyes turn away from the speaker and focus straight down the table. You know the speaker might just as well stop talking at that moment as this man's mind is made up; a decision on that point has been reached.

The impact of this is dramatic and powerful. All nod their agreement. Nobody dares to dissent. Yet, none are quite conscious why.

And who got the girl at the party? Watch that man who knows his "body language." He has moved in close to her after a slight suggestion of a smile—no, a broad grin. He is closer than ordinary. Hardly 12 or 14 inches separate their heads, instead of the usual two feet. He is in her "territory."

She knows it and feels it. But she is not offended. He has not touched her or taken any liberties.

Look at his hand now. It is resting on the bar next to hers. The glass he holds is less than an inch away from hers. Hardly improper or forward, but highly provocative. His body is saying "I like you and I want to be closer to you." She considers that he has broken the ice and she accepts it. She takes his arm as they walk out together.

To be powerful and in control of people you need to be programmed to feel that way and then your body language will help to make you that way.

Take the simple matter of posture.

You are looking for a job. You feel depressed. You walk with your head down. You may be "lost in thought" but you look "bowed in defeat." If the period of unemployment is a long one, you can recondition yourself to be naturally stooped and slumped even though you formerly stood erect. Now you are anything but the picture of success. You are the picture of failure. Nobody wants to ride with a loser, so you are breeding further defeat. Even if you do happen to land a job, your body is reflecting further defeat. Either you must recondition it or you are inviting trouble.

To have stature, you must stand tall.

To have power, you must radiate confidence.

To attract, you must reflect inner strength.

If we program ourselves right now to stand erect and to encourage our body to reflect our recent programming of self-worth and confidence, we polish the magnet and we see results.

Here are your programming instructions:

> I see myself in erect posture. I feel important and successful. My body reflects my tremendous ability in posture, movement, and position. I radiate leadership and attraction.

Do it now.

How to Get Results for Yourself from Chapter 6 Now

First program yourself for togetherness, then ...

Become aware of your own body language and that of others. Program yourself to understand what they are saying to you. But program yourself not to reflect what you don't want them to know about you.

Walk ten feet tall. Feel powerful and magnetic. Do the H-C exercises that automatically conform your feelings, attitudes and behavior to a person of stature, success and irresistible attraction. See yourself *in control.*

7 – HOW TO RELEASE IRRESISTIBLE ENERGY TO GET WHAT YOU WANT FROM LIFE

What to Expect in This Chapter

You are now going to add voltage to your H-C programming. This chapter takes you up to a new level of mind control that makes even greater things happen for you—faster.

Have you often wondered where people get all their energy from? In this chapter you will find out.

We told you earlier how you are using only a small fraction of your brain capacity and how H-C activates some of your unused intelligence. Now we are going to double that activation. It takes only a few minutes. Even if you've already seen some major changes in your life from your new programming, you haven't seen anything yet!

The degree to which you are able to relax and get finger, hand, and arm signals is the degree to which H-C programming is effective.

Double the depth of body and mind tranquility and you double the results.

In chapter 3 you learned to begin the H-C procedure by taking a deep breath, exhaling slowly, and closing your eyes gently.

This is an easy, quick way to relax. It brings immediate results. Thousands of people find this the most effective way to begin.

However, thousands more are perfectionists. If there is a better way, they are willing to put in some extra time and effort to benefit by it.

How to Magnify the Power of Hypno-Cybernetics

People all over the world seek to attain deep levels of mind—now known as alpha levels because they produce that frequency of brain waves—in order to tap the most creative brain power possible.

They use yoga, meditation, self-hypnotism, as well as hooking themselves up to brain-wave frequency feedback gadgets that indicate when the user is "there."

All methods require relaxation. First the body is eased of tension and coaxed into a state of blissful repose. The mind then tends to follow suit.

You are going to enjoy this.

You are going to experience such delightful, therapeutic unwinding that you will want to do it again and again.

Here is how it goes. After you have taken that deep breath, exhaled and closed your eyes, take an imaginary trip. Your finger will rise as usual, perhaps even before you have got very far along the imaginary happening. Let it. Perhaps the whole levitation process will be more dramatic or pronounced. But don't dwell on that. Keep your mind on the imaginary event that we will now describe:

You pretend you are having a dream. You are in a department store. You are riding down an escalator. Every floor you descend, you seem to get sleepier and sleepier. Things in the store get hazier. You feel closer and closer to the whole dream fading away. Just before it does, you give yourself your H-C instructions.

In order to make this imaginary event become more real, we will put it into words. Now these are not words you have to read as you do it. Nor do you have to memorize them. These are just words to give you the general drift of what you feel in this make-believe dream.

Read this through once so you get the general idea. Note the countdown, five to one:

> Five. I am on the escalator.... It moves slowly downward ... I see the store, the people ... Four. I am getting very sleepy ... It is a good feeling... As I go down and down I have less sensation ... Three. I drift deeper and deeper into a sleepy state ... I feel that I am floating down ... Deeper and deeper... Two. The people get hazier, less distinct... But the escalator continues to descend ... With every breath I take I go deeper and deeper ... Closer and closer to sleep... One. I have less and less sensation ... Take less and less notice of things around me... Deeper... I have no desire to move. I enjoy it very much ...

Read this through again. Notice the main points—the escalator keeps moving slowly down. You feel less and less sensation. You become drowsier as you descend. It's really quite simple.

Now the point is that you use this to create a better contact with your automatic mind. You use it before, during, or after your finger levitation—or all three. Then when you do an H-C programming the effect is greatly magnified.

Try this out by repeating the last H-C programming exercise you did, reinforcing it with this escalator technique.

Put the book down and do it now.

Energy-Limiting Commands That Program Us Daily

It would be a different kind of a life if we could turn off the input part of our mental computer until we were ready to program into it the information that we select.

This input circuit is open all the time. Even when we are asleep, we are being programmed by conversations that drift to us within hearing level.

Surgeons know that their patients hear even under full general anesthesia.

Medical case histories tell the story of the doctor on the table for a gallbladder operation. Even though under anesthesia, he over-hears the surgeon say, "The blood looks pretty dark down here." The patient, being a doctor himself, understands dark blood means a shortage of oxygen. He struggles to breathe more deeply and faster. Later, he recovers from the operation but comes down with asthma.

He does not remember any connection between the asthma and the gallbladder operation, but when he seeks help from a hypnologist, this is revealed. The asthma has become a way of reassuring himself his blood is well supplied with oxygen. He compares the louder breathing in asthma to the way he heard his breathing amplified, during the operation, by the anesthesia mask. Of course, the hypnologist reprograms him to normal breathing by ordering him not to have any more asthmatic attacks since they are no longer useful or necessary.

If conversation gets through to us in anesthesia, you can imagine how it gets through to us in sleep or in waking hours. We don't have to be listening—our computer still gets the message.

Let's say you are having your morning coffee. The television announcer has just completed the news. Now, the weather. But first an announcement. You leave the table to clear some breakfast dishes and to pour yourself a second cup of coffee as the announcer proclaims:

> Creamy Gold is the world's richest ice cream. It is brimming with nourishment, made only with natural dairy products. Buy the economical quart-size with the see-through top. Your choice of 15 tangy Creamy Gold flavors.

Your mind may have been on whether you should do the dishes

now. Or whether the coffee pot was still hot.

It doesn't matter. You are still hooked. Your mind has been programmed toward ice cream in general and Creamy Gold in particular.

Multiply these types of suggestions a hundred-fold among two-hundred million people and you could have a national obesity problem.

Multiply negative suggestions which you yourself have received since childhood a thousand-fold and it's a wonder you are doing as well as you are.

> Stay out of a draft or you'll catch a cold.
>
> Don't get your feet wet or you'll catch a cold.
>
> You stupid brat!
>
> Clumsy!
>
> You never learn.
>
> You're impossible.
>
> You won't have the time to do that.
>
> Don't go out above your head.
>
> You won't have enough capital to swing that idea.
>
> It'll never sell.
>
> You can't.

So it goes all of your life.

Can you insulate yourself from negative programming?

Yes, there is a way.

Some computers are programmed to reject certain programming. Your automatic subconscious can also be programmed to reject put-downs, limiting statements, and other failure-oriented "material."

Here is how you can do it now.

See it in your comfortable chair. Take your deep breath. Close your eyes. Begin your escalator ride and finger levitation. When really deeply relaxed give yourself the following instructions.

Negative thoughts do not enter or influence me. I reject them.

Positive thoughts bring me all the advantages I desire.

Do it now.

How a case of inferiority complex was handled

Mrs. V.A. would blush at the drop of a hat. In any face-to-face situation, she was aware of this embarrassing blushing that turned her face beet red. She began to anticipate it and that alone would bring it on. She got to be so ashamed of it she would avoid people altogether. She literally drove herself into a corner.

In discussing this problem, it became clear that she had experienced blushing since a child. She still felt it most keenly with people in authority or new people who might prove to be authoritative.

H-C was used to convince her that she was equal to other people. She had no reason to be self-conscious. She was to understand that the blushing may have been performing a function as a child, but that it was no longer needed and would indeed stop.

It did. She reported a couple of months later that ordinary face-to-face encounters with people were now totally comfortable and the blushing was no longer a problem. She said that on one or two occasions involving situations that any girl would blush at, she blushed. She asked to be relieved of blushing even under such conditions. We demurred.

A negative thought was causing this problem. "I am inferior. Don't look at me." What do the exact beginnings matter? They could be cancelled now, whatever they were.

They can also be prevented from taking hold in the first place. The previous H-C exercise is a powerful deterrent to somebody else exerting unwanted power over you. It is worth using today and reinforcing it from time to time in the days to come.

How Fear Can Sneak up on You

The beauty of this H-C exercise is that it works automatically. You don't have to realize that someone is zinging you with a negative barb to have it protect you. Its protection becomes automatic.

For instance, a flyer arrives in the mail. It is addressed to you. It is from an insurance company. It says in big black letters:

Accidental Death is the Number 1 Killer of People Under 45.

You are under 45. You are being programmed to think of accidental death as a probability. Is this what you want? There is a "personal" letter with it. It is typed by a computer-like process that inserts your name repeatedly in the body of the letter. Zing. Zing. Zing.

Many national organizations that raise funds to combat one disease or another use "scare" tactics. This is all negative conditioning. What we fear we often attract. As Franklin D. Roosevelt put it—all we really need to fear is fear itself.

Fear is a downer. So is self-criticism. Any negative thoughts— your own or "gifts" handed to you by others—act as a dam to impede the flow of your natural energy and vitality.

To make that energy and vitality flow through you as never before you need to:

1. Cancel old negative programming.
2. Block all further negative programming.
3. Activate through new conditioning.

We have taken care of the first two steps in this chapter. Now for step three.

How to Turn Up Your "Valve" for

Unlimited Energy and Vitality

A man recently terminated three years of unemployment as a machinist by taking a job as an advertising space salesman for a local newspaper. He dreaded making his first call, kept delaying his sales effort in the field, until he was risking losing this job, too.

He did one H-C exercise: When he reached his relaxed state of mental contact, *he visualized himself making his first call, having his first interview, and selling his first contract.* He did this exercise six times that first day.

When he woke up the next morning, he was so "primed" for the job that he almost flew to that first call. And he got a year's contract from the advertiser.

A stock clerk was having supervisor trouble. At the rate he was getting along with his immediate boss, he'd be a long time getting anywhere in the firm, if he could hold his job.

He did a two-part H-C exercise.

First, he asked for a feedback from his mental computer to pinpoint the sources of friction. As he sat with finger up, he relived some of the recent incidents with his supervisor. Acting as an impartial observer, he tried to spot why he himself acted the way he did, and why the supervisor acted or reacted the way he did. He had a strange feeling, while seeing this re-enacted before his eyes, that he was the son and the supervisor was the father.

This gave him the "fuel" for the second part of his H-C programming: *He saw himself as a skilled warehouse clerk. He saw his supervisor as an experienced warehouse operator.* There was a time lag of about one week during which the H-C programming was repeated daily. At the end of that week the relationship had changed from a frigid generation gap to warm, mutual respect.

The specific cases here—a reluctant space salesman and a recalcitrant stock clerk—do not very likely fit many readers.

However, the message is the same for both, and meaningful for millions of people:

The Price of Happiness

Enjoy what you are doing and life is a ball.

A gardener is raking leaves on the lawn of a large country estate. It is a tedious, boring job. No self-respecting person in his right mind would want such a job regardless of the pay. But to this gardener it is sheer joy.

Watch him in action. And listen. As he rakes, he sings.

At first you think it cannot be him singing. Perhaps somebody on the other side of the hedge has a radio going. No, it is the gardener. He is singing "I Believe" with such fervor and tone that it seems incredible he still has energy left over to rake.

The fact is he is using life energy. He probably will feel at an even higher level of energy and well-being when he finishes the so-called chore than when he started.

Energy can flow—effortlessly. That is called life energy.

Or it can be forced—only with great effort. That is called physical energy.

Whenever you block your life energy, you must use physical energy to do the job.

Then the job becomes an effort. It can look insurmountable.

Why carry water from a well in buckets when you can just turn on the tap!

If we were totally without fear ...

If we were in no ruts and had no habits ...

If we were innocent and naive and without inhibitions ...

If we were oblivious to all the requirements of, and our responsibilities to, society ...

We would be putting up no barriers to the free flow of life energy.

We would also be in deep trouble.

Fears, habits, inhibitions and prohibitions cannot be disaffirmed, denied or ignored.

But they can be understood. Some can even be circumvented. Many can be gradually transformed or dissipated.

"I have to be nice and do what is expected of me."

"I have to be sure and not hurt so-and-so's feelings."

"I have to please so-and-so."

"I have to" is quite different from "I want to." "I have to" is uphill. It takes physical energy. "I want to" is downhill. It takes no physical effort. It flows effortlessly with life energy.

If we knew we were tied down to physical energy and uphill living or working, by such an "I have to" decision, what can we do about it with H-C?

"We are discreet sheep," commented Mark Twain. "We want to see how the drove is going, and then we go with the drove."

Conformity is another way of saying "I have to." We conform with what is expected of us. Why? Because it is safer. It is a popular treadmill. We do not walk it alone.

It takes a certain amount of adventurousness to blaze your own trail, to do your own thing.

Your Key for Success

Here is the key: substitute for conformity the courage to be yourself, to do your own thing, to do what you want to do rather than what you have to do.

Make this substitution and the road becomes effortless. You have all the energy and vitality of a car going downhill. It doesn't ever need to have gas in the tank. You have energy to spare. The end of your day finds you just as lively and full of pep and enthusiasm as the beginning.

You will startle the evening bowling team and amaze your bridge table friends.

Are you willing to make the switch from uphill struggle to downhill breeze?

Here is how. Get into a deep state of relaxation. Then reprogram your automatic mind with the following visual image:

> I see myself with the courage and confidence to live and work the way I enjoy. I see myself able to be even more productive as I become free to apply my own initiative and intuition. I am creative, original and unique. I am appreciated and respected the more for it.

Ready. Go.

The Secret Ingredient You Need to Get Your Way and Make Others Like It

Most people are in a 9-to-5 rut. Look around you. Some are creatures of habit from the time they switch off the alarm at 7 a.m. to the time they switch off the television set at 11 p.m.

They have a goal. It is to do tomorrow what they did today.

They live in little boxes of time and routine. They dress the same way, go to work by the same route, buy the same food in the supermarket, and cook it the same way.

Suppose their goal was to move from where they are today to a better life tomorrow.

Would that make a change? You bet it would.

Some mornings they might want to get up early to get something done that was important to their goal, or stay at work later. Their enthusiasm and zest for life, as they worked at and for what they wanted, would be infectious. Others would "pull" for them. Help would come from unexpected sources. They would reach their goal effortlessly, perhaps sooner than they expected.

There is no greater happiness in this world than the opportunity for creative expression toward personal goals.

But first you must have these goals.

Suppose a fairy godmother appeared to you in the Cinderella tradition and offered to fulfill one wish. What would you wish?

Pause now and consider. Money. Health. Love. Of course, but be more specific. Make your wishes goal-oriented. For example, "I wish I could become an owner of this company." Or, "I wish I was the most active and influential man in this club." Or, "I would like to be elected to public office." Or, "I would like to increase my sales to seven figures and my income to six figures."

Now let this wish become your goal.

Program yourself to attain this goal.

Do it this way. In your H-C position, see yourself standing looking off to the distance. In the distance you see your goal accomplished. You see yourself moving toward your goal.

Do it now.

This "goal" exercise should be repeated every few days. As you progress, you see the picture of the accomplished goal in greater and greater detail.

As you reach your goal, set a new one. Do the same exercise with this new goal.

There is no end of goals you can reach—effortlessly. You will have more and more energy and vitality as you go along.

And others will wonder how you do it.

How to Get Results for Yourself from Chapter 7 Now

Step up your H-C control with the escalator technique. Use this higher voltage control to cancel the effect on you of negative thoughts, past and present. Then use it to switch from your expenditure of uphill physical energy to downhill life energy. Now you are ready for the "activator." Set a goal and program yourself for it. Reach it "in a breeze."

8 – HOW TO BE A LEADER IN ANY PROJECT YOU WANT TO CONTROL

What to Expect in This Chapter

In chapter 6, you programmed yourself for control over other people. In chapter 7, you intensified that programming and added limitless energy. Now. in this chapter, you get down to day-to-day happenings. You become the leader any time you want things to go a certain way. And that's the way you take them.

In 1972, the United States introduced "smart bombs" that found their way to within five feet of their Vietnam targets, thus increasing the effectiveness of air strikes against war industries and reducing civilian casualties.

They work through the use of a laser beam. This beam is focused on, say, a bridge span. Wind does not cause drift and there can be no similar error factors. The bomb has a heat sensitive device that follows the laser beam right down to the target.

Man's brain has the potential to act like a laser beam. It does not shine that kind of a light but it seems to focus on his programmed goal and take him there just as if he was locked into a laser beam.

This is a programmed book. It is a step-by-step reprogramming of your life. If you skip some of the chapters or steps within a chapter, the results cannot be as effective.

If you have followed most of the H-C programming sessions so far, you have reset your life's programming for:

1. Understanding that miraculous changes are possible through the automatic mind.

2. Contact and communication with the automatic mind through finger levitation.

3. Canceling self-limitation, "I can't" and other failure-oriented programming.

4. Substituting self-confidence, "I can" and other success-oriented programming.

5. Specific programming for cash and self-worth.

6. Body language that reflects your newfound power and control.

7. Additional voltage for more effective instructions to your mental computer.

8. Unlimited energy to do any job you want to do.

You are now conditioned for the immediate results in the next step of your H-C program.

9. Become outstandingly successful at specific projects that face you today, tomorrow, or the next day.

How to Turn on Your Laser Beam for Use any Time

Mr. S.J. had done very well in his first few years as an insurance agent. Now he had hit the million dollar mark for the year and the company was giving him an award. But he was terrified at speaking before groups. He planned to become ill a day or two before the award dinner.

He realized that this was foolish. He had goals that he wanted to reach in the company. Now was the time he must end this fear of public speaking. He could not permit it to stand in his way. He decided to use H-C under the authors' guidance.

It took five steps but they were all done in one day.

First, he visualized himself speaking eloquently to one person— a close friend or a member of his family.

Next, he visualized another person joining the conversation, while he kept his gaze fixed on the first person.

Then, he added a few more people, but he still saw only that first person as he talked.

Now, a large audience was present, but he was visualizing himself still addressing that one person.

Finally, he visualized himself doing just that at the dinner when he received the award—addressing his remarks to one person in the audience who was close to him, and paying no mind to the others.

The authors received a glowing note a few days later. It read, "I (we) did it!"

This multistep programming is just as simple as one-, two-, or three-step programming. It is done one step at a time. It is best to space the steps a few hours apart.

Why not "see" the final result in one visualizing step as we did in previous H-C procedures? Good question...

How to Get Rid of Latent Fears Holding You Back

In the example of the insurance man, he was programmed by some past experiences to be terrified of speaking to large groups. Perhaps, his parents made him stand up and say something at his four-year-old birthday party. He never saw anybody stand up and say something before. He felt singled out. Instead of tasting birthday cake, he was tasting shame and terror. Or perhaps he forgot his lines at some school play and felt like the classroom idiot as his knees trembled and his hands dripped perspiration.

Whatever the cause, the memory of that experience was still actively programming him. To give contradictory programming without first removing this would cause an anxiety producing conflict and possibly extreme discomfort.

In such a case you have two choices:

1. You can regress your memory to identify the event. Then relive it in your imagination. See how irrelevant it is for today. (This is like refiling it in your automatic mind under "inactive." Thus removing it from active programming of your behavior.)

2. You can introduce a side-stepping program which avoids direct confrontation and conflict. This is done one step at a time to confirm that no anxiety is felt. (The side-stepping aspect in the example was his talking to one familiar person.)

In a later chapter, we will give you several methods to dig out stubborn memories that are programming you against your will. They may be making you fat or skinny, angry or sad, too timid or too bold.

Once these memories are remembered, you have them by the tail.

Meanwhile, however, the side-stepping method is very useful. You move right ahead with it—no sweat.

You are able to turn on that laser and home right in on it.

Unwanted circumstances, obstreperous individuals, obstructive tactics—all melt under its hot, white light as you emerge: in control.

How to Program Yourself for Leadership

at Meetings and Conferences

Most progress in our civilization is made in the group framework.

Homo sapiens (human) is gregarious. He is not accustomed to being a loner. He works best in families, communities, organizations, companies, societies, and other types of group action.

If you are a loner and feel it is to your advantage to remain that way, fine. But read this section anyhow. Even a poet, artist, or philosopher can benefit from group action. It might help to get the poetry read, art seen, and philosophy heard by larger and more appreciative audiences.

Some people go to a meeting and disappear in the wallpaper. Others stand up and monopolize the proceedings to the point of nausea—full of sound and fury, signifying little of constructive value.

Then there is the leader. His laser shines on the target quietly, accurately. And everybody there homes in on it.

There's a funny thing about light. You cannot see it unless it hits something. You may think the rays you see are light. But that is light hitting small particles in the air. Without these particles, you can see light only when it strikes something and illuminates it.

Important Programming Secrets

When a leader shines his laser on a goal or a solution, he doesn't light up. The room doesn't light up. Only the answer everybody is seeking lights up.

No big noise. No big show. Just results.

You have a choice. You can program yourself to be a big mouth. Or you can program yourself to be a communicator.

For a would-be tennis player or golf player to program himself to be a real pro at the game, he needs to know what a real pro looks like—how he hits a serve, or how he tees off.

You are about to program yourself to be a leader at whatever level you wish—even if it's only to have the last say at home. But to be a leader even at this level, you need to know what a leader looks like, how he communicates, what he feels inside.

Visualize a person standing in the doorway. It is too dark to recognize just who that person is. But we'll tell you this much. That person is a born leader with the following attributes: (The "he" is generic. It could be a man or a woman.)

- He does his best—and then a little bit more
- He is patient and persistent.
- He has a broad view.
- He shoots for realistic goals.
- He knows how to handle people.
- He communicates well-talking and writing.
- He knows how to teach.
- He knows how to sell.
- He is a conservative when it comes to preserving the best of today.
- He is a progressive when it comes to introducing new ideas for tomorrow.

These might sound like the ten commandments for successful leadership. But consider them instead as the only ten clues that you have to recognize who that silhouette is standing in the doorway.

Your Personal Programming Progress

Now follow these directions: (A) Go to a mirror and take a long look at yourself. (B) Read the ten clues again. (C) Do an H-C programming procedure. See the silhouette of an unidentified leader in the doorway. Then see that person emerge into the light. It is you. Yes, it is most certainly you.

Do it right now.

You now see yourself in a new light. You can visualize yourself being a more effective person at:

- impromptu meetings
- formal business conferences
- community get-togethers
- family parleys
- social discussions
- political rallies
- organization deliberations
- committee huddles

Now for a step-by-step programming of your automatic mental computer to side-step all previous blocks, to enable you to zero in on the crux of the meeting, and to shine your "laser" on the solution.

How to Get Results That Win Admiration at Any Meeting

This story is told of Cyrus Ching, a distinguished industrialist. Shortly after he was appointed to the Federal Mediation and Conciliation Service, Ching found himself in a labor-management dispute that was not going well at all. The atmosphere was tense and hostile, one in which no proposal or counter-proposal could possibly be well received.

Ching turned to the union spokesman—a man named Lee—and said, "Mr. Lee, with names like ours, we should be in the laundry business together instead of wasting our time here." The prospect of a Lee-Ching laundry brought a round of laughter from everyone present. The tension was broken. Hostility was momentarily forgotten and Ching went on to bring the two sides together.

Ching was an experienced mediator. He knew he could make little progress unless everyone was ready to pull together.

"Experienced." This means he was programmed. You need to program yourself to be aware of feelings of hostility and animosity; then to contribute to that same "oneness" and rapport that you programmed yourself to feel individually in an earlier chapter.

Step #1

This is step one. Give yourself the following instructions. Do it in a deep state of relaxed communication with your automatic mind. It will act as a servomechanism, turning you on to laser-like sensitivity and accuracy.

> I am aware of differences between people. However, I am even more aware of their areas of agreement. I seek to reinforce these areas of agreement.

Use some visual image symbolic of yourself as the solon, or peacemaker. See yourself in a judge's robe or presiding as impartial chairman.

Ready? Do step one toward laser-like leadership now.

Step #2

Step two involves your own ideas—how to encourage good ideas. Then how to ease them into a family discussion or business meeting in a way that assures their being taken seriously by those present and hopefully adopted.

Chapter 13 is devoted to programming yourself to be an idea

generator and problem solver. We will cover that aspect only generally right now, concentrating more on the method of presenting your proposals in an "appetizing" acceptable manner.

Let's get something clear right now.

Programming is just that. You do not have to learn anything in this book. Do the H-C sessions and it happens automatically.

So don't feel you have to memorize anything or learn anything. The beauty of H-C is that it all happens effortlessly in your chair. You visualize in a state of repose. This, in effect, is like inserting electronic data into your computer. The rest is all taken care of right on schedule without any "remembering to do it" on your part.

We repeat this now because, as the H-C "data" that you give yourself begins to accelerate, you may get flashes of those days in school when you had to study, memorize and cram.

No way.

H-C is a doing. No "head trips" here.

When you put the book down and give your automatic mind specific instructions, consider it done.

You will automatically remember what you need to. You will behave as you are programming yourself to behave. This does not mean you will be an automaton. You will be a more capable, inspired human being.

How to Make Your Ideas Shine Attractively

Boredom is the widely prevalent characteristic among working people today. For most Americans, the hardest step all day is the first step they take on their way to work in the morning.

Sign pointers of boredom: priority of less working hours over more pay, higher turnover especially among career workers, apathy on the job, three-hour martini lunches, absenteeism. Psychoanalyst and author Erich Fromm calls boredom "the illness of the age."

Boredom is the uninvited guest at every meeting, social, political or business. It invites aggressiveness, destructiveness and obstructionism. Meetings or discussions can drift like a rudderless ship. They can go around and around in circles. They can go on and on getting nowhere because of bored, let-George-do-it attitudes.

Hello, George. Yes, from now on you are George. At least, you are the one who is going to give purpose and direction to any get-together. People will love you for it. You will be looked up to and admired.

And it will be the easiest respect you ever earned in your whole life.

We are going to paint two pictures for you.

Picture "A" is of a person who goes to a meeting or is present at a discussion, accomplishes nothing by his being there, and emerges as inconspicuously as he went in.

Picture "B" is of a person who attends a meeting or a conference, contributes to its success, and emerges with greater stature than he entered, possibly symbolically wearing the hero's mantle on his shoulders.

Picture "A"

Here is Picture "A." This person attends but he really doesn't know why. He seems to be listening, but one wonders. For most of the time, he just sits doodling, smokes cigarettes, and makes side comments to the people sitting next to him. If a groan arises, he groans, too. If there's laughter, he joins in it. He might make a statement or a proposal but it doesn't seem to set anybody on fire. When the meeting is over he leaves. Asked how it went, he gives a neutral shrug.

Picture "B

Here is Picture "B." This person has come to the meeting prepared. He knows why the meeting is taking place. He has a grasp of the purpose or problem. He has even put together a few facts on a piece of paper leading to a possible action or solution. He listens intently. He sees the golden moment to speak up. What he says is "right on." He backs it up with facts. He shuts up. Boredom disappears. People are anxious to come to a decision and the answer seems close at hand now. A consensus is taken. The meeting ends. It was a good meeting.

The difference between pictures "A" and "B"

Do you get the picture? Do you see the one big difference between the person in Picture "A" and Picture "B"?

It is *interest.*

If you are interested and other people are bored or apathetic, you are a stand-out. You are the key to making it a successful event.

If you are *interested,* you

- know your subject
- are receptive to others' ideas
- keep your eyes and ears on whoever is talking -
- give your own ideas, clearly, concisely
- accept the decision of the majority graciously

Sometimes a decision is not in favor of the idea that you proposed. No matter. You are building toward the time when it will be.

Also, there is a possibility that instead of a decision being made, there is merely an agreement to study the problem further or to get some missing information or opinions. If you are an interested participant, you either volunteer or find yourself delegated to a follow-up action.

Often a committee is appointed to get this job done. Guess who is likely to be the chairman? This is just delayed recognition. Continue your interest and enthusiasm. Your successful chairmanship of what appears to be a minor, even unimportant, committee can vault you to immense recognition in the eyes of important people.

Picture "A" or Picture "B"—in which can you see yourself?

Select Picture "B" and program yourself for it. Make sure you see your interest and enthusiasm when you hold yourself in that picture. See yourself bringing that fact sheet to the meeting. See yourself making a proposal at the "golden" moment.

Relax; get a finger levitation; deepen your relaxation with the escalator technique; use visual instructions to "automate" Picture "B."

Now.

How to Generate Ever-Widening Circles of influence with These H-C Commands for Power Expansion

Man gains power and influence when he gets together or communicates with other people. That's why the previous meeting-programming has first priority in the focusing of your laser beam.

You create a circle of influence at a meeting of any kind. From there you need to widen that circle.

As that circle widens it encompasses more and more strata of society or the business world. You get known in politics for your social welfare work. Or the sharp reporter on a newspaper gets known in the circulation department for his help to them. Or the fellow who solved the problem about the open sump at a civic association meeting gets to be sought after by the eligible women of the community.

As the circles widen, they all add up to what you want them to: sex, money, power, influence.

The power of your laser

Your laser can reach out any distance. It can burn as brightly as it needs to to accomplish your goals. Leave it to your magnificent subconscious servomechanism. You program it. It does the rest.

Here is your step-by-step programming for laser-like power in any project you want to control and for ever widening circles of admiration and influence. These steps apply to business and they apply to education. They apply to sports as well as to family relationships. They go just as well in a framework of boys and girls together as in a framework of politicos caucusing in a smoky room.

Do one step at a time even though they are listed together. Stop where you see the mark * * * and do your H-C exercise. Wait a few minutes or a few hours before you do the next.

Start now.

"I see myself as an expert communicator. I talk and write clearly and logically. I am a channel for the exchange of helpful information."

* * *

"I am dependable and efficient. I make time count—mine as well as other people's time. I have initiative."

* * *

"When I solve problems, I first get all the data. I then consider all obvious alternatives, all pros and cons, all less obvious directions. I come to a reasonable conclusion."

* * *

"I know where I am going. I see my goal or destination. People work with me, not for me, toward that goal. I see progress every-day."

* * *

"I show patience and make allowances. I understand other people's motives and purposes. I make concessions if I have to, in order to reach my goal."

* * *

"My mind retains and indexes all it needs that is important. It is harnessed and programmed for my control and success."

* * *

"I am a person of purpose—responsive, alert and maneuverable. I observe all that is going on around me. I gain advantage, wisdom and power from all that I observe."

* * *

"I see myself as an executive with the ability to make sound decisions promptly. I think quickly under pressure. I do so with courage, self-assurance and optimism."

* * *

"I am a man of action. I see myself helping others to overcome their apathy and inertia. I see what needs improvement. I make things happen."

* * *

"I inspire the best in people by the example I set myself. I am aggressive but not vain. I fight to win, not to kill. I am a winner."

* * *

You may read on but mark off these ten programming steps as you accomplish them. Come back and work them over again if you feel reinforcement would be valuable.

Shine your laser on your goal now. The higher that goal the better. The sky's the limit!

How to Get Results for Yourself from Chapter 8 Now

Review the nine steps that comprise the programming so far as listed at the beginning of this chapter. You can begin to get the broad view of how you are building your power and performance. If you detect a problem in your own personality, something that just does not permit you to see yourself as a person of influence or stature, use the "one step at a time side-stepping procedure." Apply it to your problem just as the speech-fearing insurance man applied it to his. Go on to programming yourself for laser-like leadership at meetings with other people. Finally, do the ten-step programming that sends the waves of your effectiveness surging outward to larger and larger spheres of power and influence.

9 – HOW HYPNO-CYBERNETICS ELIMINATES FEARS AND PHOBIAS BLOCKING YOUR SUCCESSES

What to Expect in This Chapter

Does something make you uneasy, uncomfortable—insects or rodents, or dark rooms, or even meeting new people or starting a new job? This chapter provides you with reprogramming instructions that wipe these unwanted fears from your mind and enable you to feel "at home" anywhere, as if you have the world in the palm of your hand.

This is a trouble-shooting chapter.

Things are going better and better every day.

But maybe they can improve at a faster rate than they are.

It's no fun to have feelings of uneasiness when walking up or down stairs, flying in an airplane, or riding in an elevator.

It's no fun to be ready for a big night and then to have it spoiled by a hang-up or a hangover.

It's no fun to move into a new life of more money, more friends, more prestige and have to take along old habits, such as nail-biting, or old phobias, such as being afraid of the water.

Fears and phobias can hinder your success. Some can even block it entirely.

Let's go trouble-shooting together. Let's identify some fear or uneasiness we might have—and maybe more than one—then go gunning for them.

By the time you get to the end of this chapter, there's no reason why you should have such problems any longer.

Nail-biting

We mentioned nail-biting. Miss Y.S. was an attractive girl—except for her hands. Her nails looked as though they were bitten down to the knuckles. Since she cared about her appearance, the H-C programming was used that projected very beautiful hands. The very first time she did this, she went for quite a period of time without putting her nails to her mouth. The second time she programmed herself for beautiful hands, this period was extended. After six times over a period of ten weeks, the period was so great that her nails had time to grow and when she did get the urge to bite them, she was able to resist consciously—for vanity's sake.

Nail-biting is a symptom of a fear or anxiety. The person who bites his or her nails may not be aware of a specific fear. Yet, it is there.

Even when we know we are afraid, we don't like to admit it to ourselves, much less to others. Yet, it can echo and re-echo in those long mental corridors of our subconscious.

Originally, pre-historic man had one basic fear—his chances of survival. This fear came in two mental apparitions—fear of danger and fear of starvation.

The general basis of our fears

Today, we have a whole world of fears to choose from: insecurity, loneliness, distrust, failure, authority, sex, responsibility, poverty, unpopularity, prejudice; and that's only the beginning.

Look carefully and you'll see that fear is at the root of alcoholism and drug addiction. It keeps people awake when they want to sleep. It drives people to excessive smoking and excessive eating. It makes them accident prone, erodes health, drains personal savings, fills hospitals and cemeteries.

Fear is at the root of all these "misfortunes" of man. Now let's see if we can find what's at the root of fear.

How to Track Fear Back to Its Source with the Pendulum So You Snuff It Out

Later in this chapter, there are specific "commands" for your automatic mind that wipe out eroding fears and phobias and replace them with strengthening courage and confidence.

But first it helps you to track fears down and see how they originated. Then you can eradicate the source and ensure that you are not creating emotional conflicts with two opposing sets of "commands" or two non-compatible mental computer instructions.

We have learned with H-C how to feed information *into* the subconscious, but how do we get information *out* of the subconscious?

There are several methods. Two involve the use of the fingers. Since your fingers have already been accepted by your subconscious mind as "lines" of communication, we will describe these two methods in detail.

One method utilizes the pendulum, the other finger signals. Both methods are used to obtain "yes" or "no" answers to the questions *you* pose to your subconscious mind. Take your pick.

The Pendulum Method

First the pendulum method. It is intriguing and fun. It goes like this.

You hold a string with a button, washer, or other weight on the end of it, placing your elbow on a table and letting the pendulum swing freely. Your wrist should be bent and your arm in a comfortable position.

As soon as you master an initial exercise to make contact with your subconscious, you are able to ask your subconscious questions like: "Did my fear (of the water) begin earlier than age 10?"

An involuntary motion of the pendulum will then occur. It may be side to side, or to and fro. By a pre-arranged code, you will read "yes" or "no" from this motion.

You continue the questioning until you have pinpointed the year, the place, the people, the event. Once you get the answer, it's like finding a pot of gold at the end of the rainbow—worth many times the small effort.

To get the pendulum working this way for you, you need to go through two initial steps that need not be repeated again.

Step One. Establishes "connection."

Step Two. Establishes a "yes," "no" agreement.

Instructions for Step One: Hold the pendulum still, in a position ready for it to swing. Close your eyes. Visualize the pendulum moving side to side. See it moving in your mind's eye. Visualize it just as realistically as you can, just the way you did in an early chapter with the shopping bag and balloon exercise. Now open your eyes to see if it is actually moving from side to side. If it isn't, keep trying. Once you succeed, visualize a back-and-forth motion, that is, towards you then away from you. Once you can obtain both these motions, without help from your conscious mind, try for a clockwise motion, then a counter-clockwise. Keep practicing until you get a fairly good swing each time, before going on to Step Two.

Instructions for Step Two: What you learned to do in Step One can now be forgotten. You do not do any visualizing to control the pendulum. It is moved by your subconscious mind from now on. However, you need to agree with your subconscious mind on a code. Which motion means "yes"? You ask this question of your subconscious mind (aloud, or just thinking the question). You hold the pendulum with your eyes closed and wait for a motion. It may be imperceptible or indistinct to start but be patient and repeat the question, if you have to, until a distinct side-to-side or back-and- forth motion results. Then ask which motion means "no"? You should now get the opposing motion from your pendulum. You now know which motion is "yes" and which motion is "no." There are two more possible motions—clockwise and counter-clockwise. Your subconscious may want to move in these directions to tell you "I don't know" and "I won't tell." Ask and find out. Sometimes the subconscious really has no experience to relate. Other times that experience is so traumatic, the subconscious refuses to divulge it, for your own good.

You are now ready to use the pendulum to track down and eliminate causes of discomfort or unwanted behavior. Let's take that case of fear of the water. It is preventing your learning to swim and your summer fun.

When and why did it start? Your questions might go something like this:

Questions Re: Fear of Water	Answers by Pendulum
Did it start before I was 15?	Yes
Did it start before I was 10?	No
Did it start before I was 14?	Yes

Did it start before I was 13?	Yes
Did it start before I was 12?	No

(You now know it happened when you were 12 years old.)

Did it happen at summer camp?	No
Did it happen at the beach?	Yes
Was the cause a big wave?	No
Was the cause a person?	Yes
My father?	No
My mother?	No
My brother?	No
My uncle Jack?	Yes
Did he throw me in?	No
Did he duck me?	Yes

You have now pinpointed the cause of your fear of the water. As you think about the time your Uncle Jack ducked you, one Sunday at the beach when you were 12 years old, you begin to remember the details.

It was a scary experience. He held your head down and you couldn't breathe. You pushed up but he held you down. Then he let you up and you gasped for breath and got some water in your windpipe. While you coughed, he laughed. You never went back in the water after that. You wouldn't go to the beach at all, if Uncle Jack was going too.

But that was a long time ago. You are an adult. No one is going to duck you now. Look at all the fun you are missing. "I refuse to let that one incident cause such fear today and interfere with my fun at the beach. It's ridiculous. I reject it."

Like water under the bridge, you are now free of that incident as a causative factor.

You are now able to give "yourself" positive instructions to enjoy the water without causing an inner conflict. These instructions appear later in this chapter.

Other Methods to Extract Secrets from the Subconscious Mind

Beryl Pfizer recently wrote, "If it's true the mind is like a sponge, I wish I could squeeze mine out once in a while and get rid of stuff I don't need any more."

That is just what we are doing. We are rooting out unwanted "stuff" that causes us to fear or to behave in a way that is not acceptable to ourselves or others.

There is another effective way to do this without a pendulum. You can use your fingers.

Here is how: Sit in your H-C position, hands on lap. Decide which fingers you will use. The thumbs on both hands for "yes" and "no," the pinkies, or the index fingers, etc. Then perform Step Two (described before), the same as you did for the pendulum, to establish which hand is "yes" and which is "no." Pick two other fingers for "I don't know" and "I won't tell." Now ask the questions the same way as described for the pendulum.

Causes of fear dissolve when exposed to the white-hot light of your own logical scrutiny. Your subconscious will cooperate with you in many ways, just as it does with the pendulum or the finger method. All you have to do is ask it.

You can ask it to remind you. Then the incident will very likely just pop into your head. You can give it a 48-hour or 72-hour time limit, and it will usually comply.

You can ask it to replay the incident back for you. Then just get into your H-C relaxation and watch an imaginary television screen. As you watch, the picture of the event will unfold.

You can even ask it to write it down for you. This is called automatic writing. It works quite well for many people. If you don't like to play the pendulum's game of "20 Questions" (or more), maybe automatic writing is for you. Here is how you accomplish it:

Sit comfortably in your H-C chair with a pad on your lap and your pen or pencil in hand. Move your hand back and forth over the pad to make sure it can move easily. Now ask your subconscious a direct question. It does not have to be aimed at a "yes" or "no" answer. It could be "What event is the cause of my fear of the water?" Look at your hand expectantly. Watch for the first sign of movement. Be patient. It will come.

When the automatic writing starts, let the movement continue until it stops of its own accord. First results may be illegible. Practice improves the readability. Repeat the question and see if the second or third try is not a distinct improvement. Sometimes writing is upside down or mirror backwards.

Patience and persistence are the key words for this method. If you feel you are not getting anywhere with this method, there is always that button on a string.

Whenever a fear's source is identified remember to relive it, re-evaluate it, and refile it.

The name of its new file category is "Inactive."

How to Shoot Down Specific Fears and Discomforts

Now you are ready to give yourself reprogramming instructions that neutralize fears, phobias and discomforts and replace them with positive outlooks and feelings of comfortable assurance.

Mr. W.S. had a fear of flying. Yet it was necessary for his business. First, he used the pendulum and found that he was nearly dropped by his father at the age of three when "horsing around" and being thrown in the air. With that out of the way, he was able to reprogram himself in three H-C sessions.

The first session he saw himself taking a plane trip step-by-step. He visualized "as if it were true" going to the airport, waiting for boarding time, getting on the plane, sitting before takeoff, takeoff, flying there, landing, getting off. He was to stop the session if he felt any anxiety along the way, then begin over in a relaxed state without anxiety.

That's why it took three sessions. He felt anxiety the first session at the takeoff. So he started over, relaxed and confident.

The second time he got as far as the landing. Again he started over.

The third time he made it. And he's been flying happily ever since.

A fear of alcoholism

A woman physician had a fear of becoming an alcoholic. She did drink some, in the evening, but she had no clear symptoms of being a problem drinker. Still the fear gnawed at her and we decided to help her use H-C to remove it. Her reprogramming instructions were used only after she identified the cause of the fear as a neighbor in her childhood who periodically caused a row that was frighteningly violent.

Her reprogramming was then very simple. She saw herself relaxed of tension; she saw herself drinking ginger ale instead of liquor alone at night; she saw herself in control whenever she did decide to have an alcoholic drink for social reasons.

A fear of elevators

A computer data processor was absolutely terrified about entering an elevator. This fear had kept him from the right jobs because he could work only in the suburbs where his office could be on the ground floor.

With a wife and two children to support, he decided to use H-C to end this condition. The origin could not be traced. Also, despite reprogramming for relaxation and self-confidence, he experienced extreme anxiety doing any H-C visualizing whenever he saw himself in an elevator.

The authors obtained detailed descriptions from elevator manufacturers of all the safety devices built into their product. These became required reading for our client. He was instructed to visualize each safety device in the elevator whenever he visualized an elevator—the cables which had a factor of safety of some four times their required strength—were to be visualized four times as thick as they really were, and so forth.

Now visualizing himself in one of these "reinforced" elevators no longer caused anxiety. He was able to continue H-C exercises without discomfort. In three days, he took an elevator ride with only minor fear. In two more days, the fear was totally eliminated. He was soon working in the city at a job that paid him three times what he was making before.

Most reprogramming to eliminate fear is extremely obvious and simple. Results are immediate. Rewards are great.

Here are some typical fears, phobias and discomforts and their counterpart reprogramming instructions:

Selected fears to be handled with reprogramming

Small rooms. "I am aware of how big the room really is. I am comfortable and assured."

Elevators. "I know elevators are safe. I use them confidently."

The dark. "The darkness is restful. I am fully relaxed in a dark room."

Meeting new people. "People are fun to meet. I gain by meeting them. I am thoroughly relaxed when I meet new people."

Strange places. "New places add to my experiences. I enjoy sight-seeing. I enjoy being in new houses, offices and situations. I am always at ease."

Different foods. "Variety in foods contributes to a well-balanced diet. I enjoy new taste sensations. I am adventuresome in my dining."

Appearing on stage. "I am oblivious of the audience. I focus on one or two people at the rear. I am totally at ease and confident."

High places. "I concentrate on the soundness and stability of where I am standing. The height expands my horizons and lengthens my view. I find it interesting. I am comfortable."

Insects and rodents. "Insects and rodents fear me. I have nothing to fear of them. I am master over such lower forms of life. I ignore them."

Dogs. "Dogs are friends. I have a live-and-let-live attitude toward them. They bark because that is their instinct. Most dogs are affectionate. I see their beauty and value."

Dirt or uncleanliness. "I enjoy a high level of resistance to disease. Cleanliness is what I desire. Uncleanliness is tolerable when I must be exposed to it."

Persecution. "People are interested in their own survival. I do not threaten anybody, nor they me. I am not the target. I go about my business in full confidence and self-assurance."

If you have any of these fears, (including fear of flying or of water discussed in the case history and example) use the programming as spelled out above in your H-C session now. If you have something else that "bugs" you, use the same formula. Put together the words and pictures that fit your case. Here are the principles to follow:

1. Instructions should be positive.

2. They should where possible state a fact that belies the fear.

3. They should reinforce the feeling of relaxed confidence.

Get your programming together. Sit in your H-C position and drop that fear right now.

The One Command That Puts You in Charge of Any Potentially Frightening Situation

Fear is a lonely trip. Color it dark gray.

It drives you apart from people until you are totally alone with your fear. You are ashamed of your fear so you tend to disguise it and build defenses around it, lest it be exposed. Exhortations by others send your fear burrowing deeper into you, where it erodes away at your personality, behavior, health and happiness. Only you can help yourself.

Chuck Medick is a sports reporter for the Long Beach (California) Independent-Press Telegram. He is also a public-address announcer for a local softball team, and a certified table tennis official.

One more thing. He's blind.

How does a blind person know that the batter has popped up or that the catcher has fumbled a pitch? He hears the difference.

Medick can hear when the pitcher throws a change of pace or when the batter has hit one hard enough to clear the fence. In Ping-pong, he can hear if the ball grazes the edge of the table. Blind since infancy, he has developed a compensating sensitivity of hearing that gives him the ability to handle many jobs skillfully.

Chuck Medick is not afraid of the dark. He is not afraid of losing his job. ("I could get a job the next day as a hospital darkroom technician.") He is not afraid, period.

Neither was a stammerer-turned-orator Demosthenes or paraplegic Franklin D. Roosevelt or dumb, deaf and blind authoress Helen Keller.

These people and thousands more who, perhaps, had reasons to be afraid discovered that fear has no foundation, that life takes care of itself.

When prehistoric man was faced with sudden danger, changes took place in his body which prepared him for a dash to safety: his blood pressure and pulse rate went up, blood sugar was raised for quick energy, and the bowels were flushed. His muscles tensed and he was ready to run.

You cannot run away from your fears

Today, man no longer can physically run from the object of his fears. But the diencephalon portion of his brain does not know this. It proceeds with all the necessary preparations for quick expenditure of energy. Net result: fluids eat away at stomach walls to create ulcers, muscles remain tense, and blood pressure stays high. A variety of illnesses can develop, such as colitis, migraine headaches, or asthma.

Maybe we ought to run when we experience fear, as when we see a mouse. It might prove healthier.

But it is far easier not to fear in the first place.

Researchers are working on psychosomatic illness in reverse. Professor Neal E. Miller of Cornell and Rockefeller Universities, with the cooperation of other scientists, is working on "operant conditioning" based on the theory that, if the mind can make you ill, it should also be able to make you well. Patients learn to slow their heart rate at will, lower their blood pressure, or calm a spastic colon.

Dr. Gary E. Schwartz, of Harvard's Psychophysiology Lab in the Massachusetts Mental Health Center, believes that "operant conditioning" can eliminate such bodily phenomena associated with fear as cold feet, sweaty palms, "butterflies" in the stomach, and heart palpitations.

How is "operant conditioning" accomplished? You guessed it. By assuming a deeply relaxed, meditative state, often described as yoga-like, but which you know to be an H-C position. This is the posture of mind-and body-control.

Let's do it. Let's get into the posture that now has become familiar and useful to us. Let's use it to eliminate fear from our life. Who needs it?

Here is the most powerful fear-melting programming you can use. Read it over several times:

> I am without fear. I have great faith in the future. I have the ability to overcome all obstacles, however formidable they may appear. I have the fullest confidence in myself. I am courageous, calm and relaxed.

Do it now.

How to Get Results for Yourself from Chapter 9 Now

Get to the sources of your fear with the pendulum or other subconscious probing method. Reevaluate the incident. Refile it under "Garbage!" Then do the positive reprogramming that moves you ahead fearlessly. For good measure, perform the "I am without fear" programming for fear-free living.

10 – HOW HYPNO-CYBERNETICS CAN QUICKLY GIVE YOU THE WINNING PERSONALITY YOU WANT

What to Expect in This Chapter

Personality is a vague area of human relations. In this chapter, it comes into clear focus. You learn how to evaluate your own personality and better yet to understand and appreciate why you are as you are. It's a revelation. But the real excitement comes as you add asset after asset to your personality and reap the amazing rewards.

Can you picture a rather attractive young woman, brunette, about 28, five-feet five? Her name is Miss A.S. She is a teacher.

Funny thing about Miss A. S. is that she cannot control her class. She cannot get along with other teachers. She has no boyfriends. Even her parents, with whom she still lives, wish she'd get the message, make a home for herself, and give them some freedom from her irritating personality.

Let's take a look inside Miss A. S. She hates her job as a teacher, hates to "hunt" boyfriends, hates to live with her folks and have to pay them for the privilege. (She contributes $30 a month for room and board.)

Yet, whenever she passes a mirror she has to stop and look at herself. For, in the mirror, she sees the perfect educator, a most attractive female, and a loving daughter.

What is the cause of the discrepancy between the ideal image in the mirror and the "sour puss" image in the world of reality? Of course, it all lies in the word "hate."

Her attitude of hate, hate, hate towards the task of teaching, the role of courting, and the responsibilities of homemaking gives her a hateful personality. Little wonder she is hard to work with, to play with, and to live with.

How a personality was changed

Can Miss A. S. use H-C to change her personality? She can and did.

She first had to admit to the difference between her ideal and her actual image. She had already done so, as evidenced by coming for H-C help to begin with. All H-C had to do was merge the two images.

Miss A. S. was asked to visualize herself in a class, conducting it magnificently, achieving student interest, maintaining student discipline, and providing valuable material to the class.

Another visual reprogramming she did was to see herself as socially active and attractive, seeing herself a charmer and being charmed.

These two reprogramming sessions, repeated several times, were so successful in changing her personality from dreary to cheery that no sessions were needed relative to her home life. Everything improved for her, right down the line.

One factor that made these sessions so successful for Miss A. S. was that she was an excellent hypnotic subject. That is, she was able to get an arm levitation on the first try. She was also able to deepen her relaxed state considerably by a count-down method.

Readers who are not satisfied with their state of relaxation or finger movement are advised to review chapter 3 and also to do the deepening exercise described at the start of chapter 7.

Another valuable review step is to master the use of the pendulum described in chapter 9. It will serve as a valuable adjunct to help you transform your personality in this chapter.

Inside every unpopular "cold" person is a warm-hearted jewel of a person trying to get out.

This chapter opens the door.

How to Identify Your Own Emotional Conflicts

We all have an emotional tug-of-war going on and maybe more than one.

They cause us to get up on the wrong side of the bed in the morning. We are short tempered. Our patience is nil. We are irritated at just about everything others do. And we tell 'em so.

These tugs within us are called emotional conflicts.

They are caused by past experiences.

They can be identified by probing our memory or our subconscious mind as we did for the cause of fears in chapter 9.

They are not as easy to identify as the specific events that trigger fears, but given a few hints you should be able to find circumstances in your past life that could be affecting your mental attitudes today.

Glance down the following list of typical emotional conflict causing factors and see if any could apply to you.

If the answer is yes, relive those aspects of your life in your memory and reevaluate them. See that they are meaningless for today. Refile them in your memory as "unimportant." In that way, you lessen and even eliminate their effect on your personality now. Later we will reinforce your newly-unburdened personality with positive H-C sessions.

If the answer is no, go over your youth and see what unique aspects, similar to those in the list below, might have had some effect on your attitudes and emotions today. Then, relive these past situations as described in the preceding paragraph.

Sources of Emotional Conflicts

Infancy and Early Childhood

1. Were you an only child?
2. Were you disciplined by physical punishment or the threat of it?
3. Did your parents constantly argue in your presence?
4. Did you feel you might be an unwanted child?
5. Were other children set before you as an example for you?
6. Did you remain overly attached to your mother or father?
7. Did you have a strict Sunday school or religious training?
8. Were you jealous of a brother or sister?
9. Were you "spoiled" by your parents?
10. Were you taught that sex was dirty or sinful?

Adolescence and "Teens"

1. Were your parents constantly bickering?
2. Was there talk in front of you about money problems or job security?
3. Were you repeatedly put down by criticism and statements that you were inferior?

4. Were you discouraged by the results you attained in your schoolwork?

5. Were you disciplined about as much as an adolescent as you were as a child?

6. Did you put your parents on a pedestal and then find that they disappointed you?

7. Did you overhear your parents in the sexual act and did this have any negative feelings for you?

8. Did you feign illness to get what you wanted from your parents, or they with you?

9. Were your parents or older brothers and sisters overly critical of you?

10. Was your home atmosphere unpleasant?

Adult

1. Did you seek to escape home by going out a lot?

2. Were your sex needs unsatisfied for long periods?

3. Did you marry at a very early age?

4. Are your sex needs, or those of your partner, unfulfilled now?

5. Are you bored with your marriage? Do you find rapport missing with your mate either intellectually, spiritually, or emotionally?

6. Are there any major differences between you and your mate, such as economic, education, mental level, economic level, basic attitudes?

7. Do you or your spouse have any physical defects that bother either of you?

8. Have there been any deaths of close relatives in your family that have caused acute mourning or depression?

9. Have there been any losses of jobs or other work prob-

lems that interfere with your peace of mind?

10. Is there anyone among your family or acquaintances for whom you hold animosity, jealousy, envy, hatred, suspicion or other negative feelings?

11. Is there a third party in your marriage, someone who is attractive to you or your mate?

12. Are your children a problem to you or a source of worry?

13. Is there a serious illness in your family or is illness being used as a hold over you or by you?

14. Is there some trouble uppermost in your mind?

15. Have you lost any large sums of money recently or in the past?

How to Use H-C to Soft-Pedal Your Personality Hang-ups

Your first reaction to reading these 35 questions is likely to be "These do not apply to me." Yet they are the source of some 80 percent to 90 percent of all personality quirks or wrinkles among Americans today.

How, then, do you use the list? Use these four steps:

First, mark the question that hits closest to "home." Then mark any others that seem to come fairly close or have some meaning for you, albeit remote. If none apply to your situation, then write your own.

Second, reserve 15 minutes to sit comfortably and think about the condition or circumstances recalled by the question. Admit that it has affected your life, your temperament.

Optional second step. If you cannot recall circumstances, assume your H-C position, get a finger levitation, and ask your subconscious to take you back to those days. Sit for a few minutes in patient reverie before you end the session with the count of three.

Third, be aware of what emotion or attitude is induced by your recollections or reveries. Do you feel anger, remorse, bitterness, jealousy, hate, frustration, inadequacy, insecurity, envy? (See lists below.) Step away and look at yourself objectively. Identify the negative culprit.

Fourth, do an H-C session with the following reprogramming instructions:

"I cancel feelings of _____ (insert what you have identified in Step Three). They are the results of _____ (insert past incidents identified in Step One) which no longer is (are) important to me. Instead, I feel _____ (insert positive counterpart to negative attitude identified in Step Three. Select counterparts from list of attitudes below or from the next list of ten personality traits).

Negative Attitudes and Positive Counterparts

Negative	*Positive*
Anger	Serenity
Remorse	Forgiveness
Bitterness	Benevolence
Jealousy	Forbearance
Hate	Love
Frustration	Satisfaction
Inadequacy	Self-esteem
Insecurity	Confidence
Envy	Magnanimity
Dejection	Enthusiasm
Resentment	Compassion
Disillusionment	Optimism
Discouragement	Encouragement
Doubt	Certainty
Bereavement	Redemption

Depression	Elation
Confusion	Calmness
Retaliation	Reconciliation
Suicidal	Survival
Disgust	Sympathy
Indignation	Charity

Ten Common Personality Traits and Their Counterparts

1A. *Rigid:* insists that things be done the way he has always done them; does not adapt his habits and ways of thinking to those of others; nonplussed if his routine is upset.

IB. *Adaptable:* flexible; accepts changes of plan easily; satisfied with compromises; is not upset, surprised, baffled or irritated if things go differently from what he expected.

2A. *Emotional:* excitable, cries a lot (children), laughs a lot, shows affection, anger, other emotions, to excess.

2B. *Calm:* stable, shows few signs of emotional excitement of any kind; remains calm in dispute, danger, social hilarity, etc.

3A. *Unconscientious:* somewhat unscrupulous; not too careful about standards of right and wrong where personal desires are concerned; tells lies and is given to little deceits; does not respect others' property.

3B. Conscientious: *honest;* knows what is right and generally does it, even if no one is watching him; does not tell lies or attempt to deceive others; respects property of others.

4A. *Unconventional, eccentric:* acts, dresses differently from others; has somewhat eccentric interests, attitudes, and ways of behaving; goes his own, rather peculiar way.

4B. Conventional: *conforms* to accepted standards, ways of acting, thinking, dressing, etc.; does the "proper" thing; experiences distress if he finds he is being different.

5A. Prone to jealousy: begrudges achievement of others; upset when others get attention, and demands more for himself; resentful when others are in spotlight.

5B. Not jealous: likes people even if they do better than he does; is not upset when others get attention, instead joins in praise.

6A. Inconsiderate, rude: insolent, defiant, "saucy" to elders (in children); ignores feelings of others; gives impression he goes out of his way to be rude.

6B. Considerate, polite: deferential to needs of others; considers others' feelings; allows them before him in line, gives them the biggest share, etc.

7A. Quitting: gives up before he has thoroughly finished a job; slipshod; works in fits and starts; easily distracted from main purposes by stray impulses or external difficulties.

7B. Determined, persevering: sees a job through in spite of difficulties or temptations; strong-willed; painstaking and thorough; sticks until he achieves his goal.

8A. Tough, hard: governed by fact and necessity rather than sentiment; unsympathetic; does not mind upsetting others if that is what has to be done.

8B. Tender: governed by sentiment; intuitive, empathetic, sympathetic; sensitive to feelings of others; cannot offend.

9A. Egotistical: blames others whenever things go wrong; often brags; quick to take credit when things go right; has a very good opinion of himself.

9B. Self-effacing: blames himself (or nobody) if things go wrong; reluctant to take credit for achievements; may think highly of himself but is not inclined to tell others.

10A. Languid, fatigued, slow: lacks vigor; vague and slow in speech; is slow in getting things done.

10B. *Energetic, alert, active:* quick, forceful, active, decisive, full of pep, vigorous, and spirited.

He Might Call Me 'Stinky'

A photographer used H-C to rid himself of feelings of inferiority.

He described the "before" condition and the results so realistically that we share his report here:

> The jangling, raucous, disturbing sound of the telephone shattered the peaceful thoughts of planting a beautiful garden on a beautiful spring day, miles away from a dirty, unkind, inconsiderate, noisy city.
>
> "Tony? Roger here!"
>
> "Hey, haven't seen you in a long time! How are you?" I replied.
>
> Being a big-time art director in a big agency in a big city, he did not have time for human talk. He jumped in with, "Got two models ready to book, an apartment lined up on East 81st. Can you shoot on Wednesday at 2:30?"
>
> "Hold on a minute and let me check my schedule," I replied.
>
> I put him on hold, took four or five deep breaths and massaged my suddenly stiffened neck. I couldn't hem or haw or present a nervous voice to this hotshot guy. He might call me "stinky."
>
> I pushed the button and put him back on the line and bravely said, "Roger, I can do it. What are we selling and what's the theme?"
>
> "Harvey's Bristol Cream, sexy boy-girl stuff. Call me later for details."
>
> Calm down, stomach; get back on my shoulders, head, before you hit the ceiling, I thought. For the next two days, I would have to go over many, many details to be ready to do a highly successful photograph so I could please everyone from Roger through the myriad of people all the way up to the client's wife in England.
>
> At this moment my mind would not function, I was bathed in perspiration. Mentally, I doubled over to form my body in the

shape of a fetus so I could slip back into the womb where I was so safe.

I enjoy my work, mostly when I hear "Great job, Tony. Send the bill." I wanted every job to be greater than the last because I didn't want to be called "stinky."

It is quite a revelation to me that after Hypno-Cybernetics my attitude toward my work has changed to a feeling of eagerness and excitement.

I am now selling myself. I have no agent to be my buffer to the many art directors in the business. I take the bull by the horns and say to them, "I can solve your problems and make you a hero." Before Hypno-Cybernetics that would have been impossible. I can travel to an appointment and have it broken by a sudden meeting or whatever and not feel it is a personal insult.

I can now enjoy a crackling fireplace for what it is, a warm, comforting experience and not as a tool for peaceful oblivion. I can enjoy an alcoholic beverage for its taste and refreshment and not something to relax my throbbing stiff neck. I can stare into a tree and enjoy the antics of the birds without looking so hard as to become a bird myself. I can enjoy Saturday and Sunday without fear of Monday and Tuesday.

My goal for the future is to be able to control my mind and body through Hypno-Cybernetics to the best of my ability. With this skill my life will be fuller and richer regardless of my circumstances. With renewed confidence I will be able to do anything I want to, without a traumatic fear of failure.

With the debilitating shackles removed from my subconscious I can realize my full potential as a human being. Through hypnosis I can better understand what makes me tick, and with that knowledge I should be able to understand what makes other people tick. And "people" is what it's all about.

Anthony C.

This is an inside story.

It is how the photographer pictured himself.

From the outside, that is if you had met him, you would have sensed a personality problem—a backing-off type of a person whom some may have called "shy" but whom others might label a "loner." He was certainly the kind of a person with whom few people could get friendly. Until...

His H-C sessions were devoted to inventorying his assets and reinforcing his self-confidence to the point where he knew he could "do anything... without a traumatic fear of failure."

He programmed himself from "loner" and "loser" to "winning" and "winner."

How to Play Up Your Personality Assets

When a person fixes his mind on the possibility of a fall from a high perch instead of the solidity of his stand, he becomes afraid of the height.

When a person fixes his mind on the shortcomings of his body instead of the talents and capabilities of his mind, his personality shrivels.

Personality thrives and blossoms when the conscious accent is on assets, not liabilities.

You have personality. It is a great personality. We don't care who you are and what you or others think of you-today, for tomorrow the Sun will rise on a new you.

All you need to take is one H-C step. It goes like this.

- List your personality assets.

- Program yourself to "dwell" on these assets.

To help you take an inventory of your strong points, sixty types of personality assets are listed below. Check off as many as seem to apply to you.

Where in doubt, use time as the measuring factor. If "I finish what I start" applies to you most of the time, credit yourself. If it applies only occasionally, go on to the next.

Personality Inventory

My moods are stable and change only with good reason.

I seldom say things that I am sorry for later.

I am popular with most people I know.

I save for the future.

I am punctual for appointments.

I can handle crises or difficulties.

I find it easy to make decisions.

I change jobs infrequently.

I am usually successful in what I undertake.

I don't easily get discouraged.

I finish what I start.

I abide by most social conventions.

I keep my word.

I am gratified more by achievement than admiration.

I am willing to take advice.

I do most things reasonably well.

I concentrate on the job at hand.

I plan for each day.

I am not "thrown" by what other people think of me.

I do not lose my temper easily.

I am not suspicious, jealous or vengeful.

I meet new people easily.

I am poised.

I do not get stage fright when in front of other people.

I do not get upset over reprimand or criticism.

I enjoy other people's success.

I am sure people will like me.

I recognize my own abilities.

I welcome people watching me at work.

I have feelings of self-worth.

I seldom worry.

I enjoy self-confidence.

I am clear as to what I want.

I set goals.

I have high hopes for the future.

I relax easily.

I am not "bugged" by pangs of conscience.

I seldom get cross at others.

I am patient with people.

I am a non-worrier.

I do not bother others with my complaints.

I usually feel energetic.

I am generally in good health.

I sleep well.

I have a healthier appetite.

I enjoy affection—both giving it and receiving it.

I make good use of my spare time.

I am able to concentrate when I need to.

I make lists of things requiring my attention.

I never put off to tomorrow what I can do today.

I drink either not at all or in moderation.

I am a good conversationalist.

I participate well in group activities.

I am a good mixer.

I recognize my own physical attractiveness.

I am a tidy person.

I dress and groom myself attractively.

I speak and write fairly effectively.

I make a good appearance.

I have a good opinion of myself.

Most personality tests provide a means of comparing yourself to others, that is to the norm.

This is not a personality test. It is a list of common personality attributes. It is self-judged. To say that the person who checks off 20 out of 60 is below or above average is reckless. Some people judge themselves harshly, others generously.

Suffice it to say that if you have checked off *one* asset, you have something to "play up."

That is what we now intend to do—program ourselves to dwell on our personality assets, rather than our lacks.

If you have checked the book, read over the assets you have checked. Then put the book down open to the list. If you have not wanted to deface the book, you have probably created a list of your assets on a piece of paper. Read this over again, and place it down on the floor near you.

Now do your H-C programming as follows:

> I am more and more aware of my personality strong points. As my awareness of them grows, so do they, and I acquire more of them. Every day in every way I become more winning in my ways.

Reread your strong points, relax, and visualize.

How to Add Strong Points to Your Personality Easily, One at a Time

Are there any strong personality factors that you would like to have been able to check as belonging to you, but could not in all honesty?

Check them now. They are going to become yours one at a time. Use a different colored pen or pencil or make a different mark or a different list.

Program yourself every morning to be what you would like to be. Add new sparkle to your personality as you add new facets.

Do you feel embarrassed about giving affection to others, or receiving affection? And do you wish this wasn't so? Then program yourself with that trait from your list:

"I enjoy affection—both giving it and receiving it." Why not do that right now.

Keep adding new positive traits to your personality. Program yourself for the whole list if you wish. Then add a few other winning traits that are not on the list.

You will actually appear different to others. They will comment on the improvement without being able to put their finger on it. ("Haven't you lost some weight?")

People will be attracted to you, without knowing why.

You will make new friends.

The usual day at work will become an unusual day as special good things happen, again and again.

You will have a luminous personality, winning ways, and a growing reputation for being an upstanding and outstanding individual.

It will be a personal triumph.

How to Get Results for Yourself from Chapter 10 Now

Use the emotional conflict chart to identify sources of personality impairment. Relive these sources to dissolve them. Then reprogram with their positive counterparts. Turn up the voltage of your personality assets by programming yourself to be aware of them. Add more personality assets, at least one a day, until you shine like a star.

11 – THE SIX STEP PROGRAM THAT VIRTUALLY GUARANTEES ACHIEVING YOUR GOALS

What to Expect in This Chapter

Expect a miracle. Expect to see yourself getting everything that you wish and that you program yourself for. Do the first programming of the plan, accept it, and practice it as you read the chapter so that you can be ensured you are on your way. Then read the rest of the chapter so that you are prepared to set new goals and create new miracles in your life.

"Great minds have purposes," remarked Washington Irving, "others have wishes."

The noted British prime minister, Benjamin Disraeli, added "The secret of success is constancy to purpose."

In this chapter we translate our wishes into specific purposes—goals that we can be automatically programmed to attain.

Then we assure "constancy to purpose" by programming ourselves to keep on the track, step after accomplished step.

This is Hypno-Cybernetics at its fulfilling best.

Like the computer programmed to take a spacecraft to Mars, we, too, seem born with a mission. Yet, many of us spend our lives in a rut, never really living up to our highest hopes for ourselves. Remove the "rut" from our programming, substitute "goal," and we take off like a bird freed from a cage.

When the computer guided the first spacecraft to Mars, it doesn't "know" that it was never done before. It doesn't hem and haw, scratch its head, or worry about whether it can do it.

The same with our subconscious computer. Its nervous system, like the electronics system, cannot tell the difference between something programmed to be done for the first time or something programmed to be done for the millionth time. It's just as automatic for it to make us head of the firm we have been working for as to wake us up at 6:30 a.m. for the thousandth time.

Want to program yourself to be a big man in politics within five years? Your subconscious mind accepts this imaginary goal as the real thing. You had better be sure this is what you want, because, mister, you're going to be making speeches and kissing babies, like it or not.

Want to program yourself to expand your private medical practice to gross $250,000 within three years, to double your company's profits within two years, triple your insurance sales within one year? Your subconscious mind doesn't drag its feet. No ifs, ands, or buts. You do it.

The Magic of Pretending

"How can I see myself becoming the superintendent of this school system when I've been a phys-ed teacher for 18 years?"

"Can you pretend you are the superintendent-to-be?"

"Well, sure I can pretend but where's that going to get me?"

It got him the superintendency.

A young lady was having difficulty getting even the slightest use out of a finger, the first time she tried to get into a relaxed, hypnotic state.

"It won't budge," she insisted.

"Well, then move it slightly. Pretend your subconscious did it."

The pretense worked. In a few sessions, her whole arm was levitating and she was getting excellent H-C results.

The power of controlled imagination

Many a pretender to the throne in history remained the accepted sovereign. Pretend, and you become. Here is why.

When you play act, you have to use your imagination. Using the imagination programs your behavior. Remember that imagined shopping bag over your wrist actually lowered your arm due to the pretended weight.

Imagine, now, that you took a steak out of that shopping bag and put it on a red-hot frying pan. Can you hear it sizzle? Does your mouth water? Chances are you have had to swallow as the saliva flowed, just imagining a sizzling steak.

Pretending triggers the imagination.

Imagination creates behavior.

Behavior forms habits.

These three steps happen every day. The tragedy of human history is that it has been largely fear-and-failure-oriented. People imagine failure and proceed to live up to their imagination.

You can turn it all around.

Pretend you are a millionaire, or a great lover, or a university professor.

Can you see yourself in such a role in your imagination?

Now can you begin to feel the past? Feeling is the beginning of behavior. Behavior is the beginning of habit.

Pretend, now, that you are able to set any goal you set your heart on—and reach it.

What would that goal be? What do you really want, Bill, Jane, or whoever you are?

If you like to write in books, write your goal down on this page. If not, take a three-by-five card or a regular sheet of paper and write your goal at the top.

Realize a Modest Goal at First

Some people hitch their wagons to a star. Your goal does not have to be sky high. It can be a modest goal such as:

- Finding a husband (or wife) in the next year.
- Moving to a home of your own within six months.
- Getting a better job in the next 30 days.
- Having a manuscript accepted within four months.
- Being an "A" student next semester.
- Making the varsity team next year.
- Winning a beauty contest within 18 months.

Sky high or hedge high, your goal will be reached.

Note that all the goals spelled out above include a time limit. You need to program a time factor into your automatic mind. How else will it know when to perform? A no-time limit goal is really not a goal.

Have you created a goal?

If you have, get ready to put the book down and enjoy a minute or two of the best fun you've had all week. You are about to pretend that your goal is reached.

See yourself there. Notice how it feels. Go through the motions in your mind's eye. Smell the smells. See the colors. Pretend it is real.

For instance, if your goal is setting up a business of your own, visualize the place of business. If the deadline was a year, imagine a calendar with that date on it. See your desk, the telephone, the rest of the office. See the work being done, the services or products delivered.

Review your goal. Put the book down. All vision this time. No words:

> (Pretend your goal is reached)... (See it)... (Sense it) ... (Take it all in) ... (Create the details)... (Know it is so)... (Enjoy it)... (Act it out in your imagination)...

Begin.

How to Put Yourself in the Driver's Seat and Get Where You Want to Go

You have just programmed the first of six steps that virtually guarantee success in reaching your goal. These steps are: 1) Plan, 2) Accept, 3) Practice, 4) Reinforce, 5) Apply, 6) Expect.

You have a *plan.* You are programmed to reach for it. You must now *accept* its attainment.

That can sound silly on the face of it. Why would anyone visualize what he wanted in life and then have to convince himself he will accept it when it arrives?

How J.D. saved his failing business

J.D. had a hardware store. Hardware stores were no longer making out. J.D. saw the handwriting on the wall. He knew he had to switch. He heard of other hardware stores taking on small household appliances—electric hair driers, kitchen blenders, clocks, coffee makers, waffle irons, barbeques, and the like.

He invited appliance dealers to send their salesmen. But when the salesmen arrived, he turned the same deaf ear to them as he had been turning to the diehards who kept trying to sell him kegs of nails and other hardware that he couldn't sell.

J.D. was not accepting his own idea. He needed to program himself that it was an idea worth moving ahead on. He used H-C to do this. It wasn't long before the screw bins moved out, the newest in labor-saving appliances moved in, and the customers rediscovered the store.

People who don't accept their own goals are constantly programming themselves not to act. It does not matter what the reason is. It all adds up to zero.

They see "I can." Then they say "I can't." And their automatic mind reports, "Does not compute."

Once you program yourself to *accept* your goal, something quite important happens to your behavior. It begins to evidence "inner drive."

Inner drive puts you in the driver's seat. It gets you where you want to go.

To others it looks as if you are expending a great deal of energy, as if you have an overactive thyroid. Only you are "in" on the secret. It is effortless. It would take a great deal more energy to stop.

What is really happening is that your automatic mind is concentrating all your natural talent, creativity, knowledge, and intuition on your goal. You are being moved in its direction, effortlessly.

Remember, this does not happen without "acceptance." Here is how to program yourself through that second step.

> I accept this goal as natural and right for me. It is the life-style I desire. It is me being myself, expressing my true nature. I aim for it.

I reach for it.

Get to a deep state of relaxation on this one. Use your H-C count-down technique if necessary. Then, program away. Now.

How to Bring Even the Most Far-Sighted Goals within Your Grasp

Your goal is etched into your automatic mind.

Acceptance of this goal has started your motor.

Now you are ready to move.

The longest trip and the shortest trip have one thing in common —they both start with the first step.

Your first steps make you realize that no matter how long-range your plan is, there is no doubt that you will reach it.

Practice in visualizing, then making progress, makes progress a habit.

You now need to visualize that first step and then to take it. Then, the next step, and take it.

There's no "can" or "can't" involved here. It's a question of whether you want it or don't want it. Your goal is something you want to reach, so reach it you will.

There were nearly 100,000 jobs going begging in Great Britain at a time recently when there were one million, unemployed. The jobs that nobody wanted were in hotels and restaurants—chambermaids, porters, waiters, waitresses. As to these kinds of jobs, the British are snobs. They don't want such servile work. Who is filling them? On the continent, waiting on tables is considered an honorable profession. So is housekeeping.

So these jobs are being filled by the people who want them —Greeks, Italians, Turks, Spaniards. They are achieving their goals.

You want. What is your first step toward getting what you want?

Here is a first step that applies to most any goal you have: Do more.

A person who does as little as he can get away with in a job is working against himself.

It is the person who does more than he has to who moves ahead.

Resolve to work more time, seek more responsibility, do something that needs doing that nobody has seen fit to do.

Do more applies to other than job goals, too. You can do more to enhance your home, your attractiveness, your abilities.

Program yourself to do more and you will be impelled to do more. Do an H-C session right now. Take 30 seconds to see yourself doing a specific extra thing toward your goal. Cleaning an office file, writing a special letter, straightening a closet, meeting a particular person, phoning, investigating, learning—all are valid first steps.

Deeply relaxed, see the image, ready, begin.

As soon as you have accomplished the first step, apply the "do more" principal again. Come up with a second step toward your goal. Do an H-C session that programs you to do it now, as you did just now. Same with a third step, fourth step, and so on.

You may not be able to look ahead more than one step at a time. But as each step is realized, you will become aware of the next. This will sound familiar to mountain climbers.

And just like a mountain climber, you will enjoy the view from the top.

How to Reinforce, Strengthen, and Ensure Your Success

You are now an experienced H-C programmer. You have a sophisticated mental computer that can handle any program you give it.

You can see how others need to program themselves out of "I can't" attitudes.

You can see how others need to program themselves with a better self-image.

You can see how others think in terms of failure, obstacles, and pitfalls.

You have been there, too. But you are not there now. You have programmed yourself to see the glass as half full, not half empty. You see yourself with unlimited potential. You no longer think in terms of obstacles. You think in terms of challenges and success.

However, the environment is still throwing brickbats at you. You are still hearing negative programming, possibly from your mate, your friends, your teachers, your co-workers.

You need to reinforce your own positive programming.

You do this in three ways:

1. You reinforce your insulation against negative suggestions from the outside.

2. You strengthen your own positive suggestions for goal attainment.

3. You ensure your success by programming yourself to fight for goal attainment.

Let's examine these steps.

Step One means to do an H-C session like one you did before. Your programming in effect is: "I am not affected by failure thoughts of others. Negativity bounces off me. Positivity I accept."

Step Two is a repeat of the goal suggestions you did earlier in this chapter.

Step Three is a self-administered pep talk like one the coach gives in the locker room between halves of a football game. "OK, team, we're going in there like bears. We're going to give it everything we have."

The willingness to fight for a goal is powerful programming. The fighting spirit makes you come more alive. In fact, police, doctors and others who attempt to talk down a suicide attempt use this technique. They try to get the person fighting mad. Put fight into him and you put the will to live into him.

The coach knows what he is doing. He knows from experience that a team, fighting mad, is a better team.

Go into your H-C state for this one with the shortest programming yet: "I fight to achieve my goal."

Do all three steps now.

Acceleration with Imaging Power

Apply is the fifth of our six steps.

Apply what? Apply yourself? That's the old way. Hard work, sweat, long hours. That's the physical energy way.

Hypno-Cybernetics is the new way. It offers you the life energy way to apply yourself. No sweat. It's like applying your foot to the gas pedal.

You use your imagination in H-C. It is man's most formidable mental power. It programs. It creates.

You can also use your imagination to program yourself to create. This applies the accelerating power to your progress.

Suppose you were to take your eyes off this page and look at the ceiling, close your eyes, and visualize yourself moving toward your goal. What do you see yourself doing? Try it.

Did you come up with something. Move to another city? Buy some new clothes? Invite the boss for dinner? Propose a new system? Take a course?

Jot down the ideas you came up with.

Now do the same in your H-C relaxed state. Visualize yourself moving toward your goal. What do you see yourself doing.

Do it now.

You should have come up with new ideas that did not come through the first time. H-C taps new problem-solving areas of the brain.

Gael Himmah is sometimes known in real estate circles as the "master lister" and is certainly a master salesman. In his early 40's, he is already retired, owns his own airplane, has written several books, owns a ranch, has started a publishing company, and has title to a fortune in real estate.

Speaking recently before a group of 200 real estate brokers and salesmen, he explained human success in terms of cybernetics. "You can program yourself to be successful by setting sub-goals for yourself." He explained how, in real estate, this means starting off with simple matters that are easily accomplished. "This establishes a successful manner of performance," he said.

Success breeds success, he is saying, but giving this old adage more scientific validity.

Himmah also understands and uses body language. He knows people well enough to stand a distance away from them, out of their "territory," or else you turn them off, he says. He knows that if a person crosses his arms or rubs his nose you better take a different tack because he isn't agreeing with you. On the other hand, if he pulls his cuffs or pats his hair, you're "in."

Kinesics, otherwise known as body language, is only one of many areas in which Gael Himmah became proficient on his way to the top. He practiced perseverance, developed an understanding of psychology, delved into economics and financing. He tried his hand at ad writing, studied sociology. Most of all he learned to understand people.

Does his experience give you any clues?

Apply your foot to the gas pedal today. Do something that will accelerate your progress. Learn something. Start something. Do something.

It can be talking to a girl, or buying a business magazine, or stopping in to chat with a competitor, or joining a country club.

Get rolling.

How to Compound Power, Wealth and Popularity

Back in 1953, a Tokyo businessman figured that transistorized radios would be just the right product for his newly-created company. It took a year or more to get the product designed, manufactured and promoted but soon his goal of substantial profits was reached. Did the Sony Corporation stop there? No, it added product after product and reached new goal after new goal until today it does an annual volume of billions of dollars.

The goal you set now may seem almost too bold, even unrealistic. But you have a powerful ally working for you. H-C will take you there faster than you think.

Then what?

Can there be even greater goals reached? Of course, and you don't even have to read another chapter to have the technique to attain them. Just start this chapter over again with a new major goal, and fit new sub-goals. Do the same six steps: Plan, Accept, Practice, Reinforce, Apply, and Expect. Expect to get there every time. Expect some progress every week.

Expectation primes your automatic mind. It reminds the computer that you are awaiting action. And it responds.

You can also program your automatic mind to create in you an expectant attitude:

> I expect results. I expect progress whether I can see it or not. My expectations are high.

How to Get Results for Yourself from Chapter 11 Now

Set a goal. Plan sub-goals. Use H-C sessions to program yourself for reaching them. Accept these goals with "I can" sessions. Move up the ladder. Reinforce your programming if and when needed. Go on to higher and higher goals.

12 – HOW TO REVITALIZE YOUR SEX LIFE WITH HYPNO-CYBERNETICS

What to Expect in This Chapter

Expect a frank discussion of sex, of male and female hang-ups that stand in the way of full sexual enjoyment. You will be able to program yourself for full sexual performance every time, greater sexual feelings, and all the sex power you need for repeated enjoyment.

A woman went to a doctor for treatment of her inability to reach orgasm in intercourse. She was given the Bryan Word Association Test from which there developed a relationship among three words— orgasm, bird, and death.

She was placed under hypnosis and recalled that when she was a girl she masturbated on the arm of a chair. Once when she did this, she reached orgasm and almost immediately stepped on her pet canary, which was hopping on the floor at the time, killing it.

Hypnotic suggestions were given her drawing a clear distinction between orgasm and clumsiness, and the problem was solved.

This case history received national attention when it was published recently in a popular magazine. It clearly revealed the potential of hypnotism to restore sexual happiness when there was programmed interference.

What is still not generally known is that the use of hypnotism, H-C in particular, can revitalize your sex life, moving it to a higher level even if it is sublime now.

The subject of sex is shrouded in bed sheets and cloaked with inhibition. If you are willing to be adventurous, frank and understanding with your partner, this chapter offers some fascinating rewards.

Sexual Benefits of H-C Programming

Women can find that H-C helps them to:

- Release vaginal fluids prior to coitus for enhanced satisfaction.

- Sensitize areas not presently benefiting from sexual contact.

- Slow up, or accelerate, the period of time necessary for orgasm.

- Heighten the sensory peaks in orgasm.

Men can find that H-C helps them to:

- Reduce or heighten organ sensitivity.

- Shorten or lengthen period leading to orgasm.

- Increase erectile rigidity.

- Increase frequency of desire.

Both men and women can find that H-C helps them to:

- Dissolve feelings of guilt or inhibition for greater enjoyment of each other.

- Give the act of love a more significant role in their total relationship.

You May Have it Good in Bed But It Can
Be Worlds Better with H-C

Many men think they know all they need to know about sex because they are aware of that part of the female body that receives the penis. For them the sex act is little more than intra-vaginal masturbation—to relieve their own sex drive rather than please their partner.

Many women also think they know it all. Yet they may be experiencing only part of the spectrum of female orgasm, or possibly none at all. For them, the sexual act can often become an obligation rather than an ecstasy.

Ignorance can play havoc with sexual pleasure.

H-C can play havoc with ignorance. It can move you out of sexual ruts up to new levels of exquisite pleasure.

An adolescent girl compares her breasts to others, wondering why they are not as large as some women's, or she imagines that her vaginal opening may be too small and that sexual relations may be painful.

An adolescent boy compares himself to his friends and worries about the size of his penis. Years later, he is still worrying whether he will be able to give sufficient pleasure to his partner, compared with his predecessors.

These are more than idle concerns. They can become deep-seated anxieties that gnaw away, eventually leaving scars in sexual behavior and attitude.

Once a light is turned on in the dark room of sexual ignorance, once men and women overcome their reticence to discuss sexual matters with their family doctor (and he gets over his own discomfort at talking about sexual matters with his patients), and once the feelings of mid-Victorian guilt are at last left behind, the pleasure level rises.

Take the girl just mentioned. She learns that the vagina dilates and expands, that it can easily accommodate the penis as well as a baby's head. And the boy learns that the size of the penis has little to do with the stimulation it can provide an aroused partner, and that a smaller penis in a relaxed state can "catch up" to a larger penis in a state of erection. The "clouds" that interfere with total enjoyment are thus removed.

Step number one in raising your level of sexual enjoyment using H-C: program yourself to be open to more and more knowledge about the anatomy of sex, to take off your blinders and look around. Books and magazine articles on sex and sexual technique are becoming common reading fare. As a topic of conversation, it is becoming less and less taboo.

The specific words are (but be sure to "see yourself' living up to them):

> I seek more knowledge about sexual matters. I have a wholesome attitude toward sexual enjoyment. The more I learn, the more I attain my rightful level of sexual enjoyment.

Guilt as the Hex on Sex

Sex has a hex on it – Guilt. One wonders whether Queen Victoria was herself as sexually inhibited as the women of her reign. In the early 1900's, sex was supposed to be a one-sided affair. Women were looked down upon if they sought sex or enjoyed it.

Today, kissing in public is looked at askance in India. Yet, in Sweden, when a magazine shows two people in the act of coital love, nary an eyebrow is raised. One country considers it wrong for a woman to bare her face. Another country defends total nudity. In a city, one mother insists that her 18-year-old daughter be chaperoned on a date, while a few blocks away another mother insists her 18-year-old daughter be fitted with a birth control device.

What is wrong? What is right? There will probably never be

total agreement on this, as everybody reacts differently to it. Depending on geographical location, family bringing up, religious affiliation, and social environment, every person has a different emotional profile when it comes to sex.

If you argue with another person on the subject, one or the other of you is bound to instill a feeling of guilt in the other. Guilt leads to inhibition. Inhibition blocks normal sexual enjoyment.

Here is a totally visual programming you can give yourself to help remove the "dirt" from sex. Attain a deep state of blissful relaxation. Get your finger levitation.

> See yourself looking at your sexual partner. You are both undressed. However, there is pane of glass between you. It is smudged with ignorance and guilt. You can hardly see each other. You begin to wipe the glass to clean it. So does your partner. Gradually the glass becomes crystal clear. You see each other clearly and sharply through this now sparkling window of sexuality.

The Need to Be Yourself in Sexual Relations

Most of the games people play are sex games.

Many men act like rapists. They confuse brusqueness and dominance with masculinity. "Only a sissy is romantic."

Many women act like blocks of stone. Inside, they are really temptresses. But they feel they must pretend to resist.

Some people make love only on Saturday night.

Others need to get "loaded" first.

Still others like to have a fight first, and then make up.

Patterns in love making can become rigid habits. Sexual ruts. Like playing it safe and ordering chop suey or chow mein every time you go to a Chinese restaurant.

If you can be yourself in sexual relations, you are a free person. Sound familiar? Being oneself is, we learned in an early chapter, a key to success in many other aspects of living.

Step One in "being yourself" is to identify your sexual hang-ups, track down the events in your past life that cause them, relive them to dissolve them or, if too painful, use H-C to neutralize them.

An unresponsive wife may have had an unpleasant sexual experience in early life. A girl of 12 is fondled sexually by her uncle. A 10-year old girl is frightened by a neighbor who exposes himself to her and offers her candy. A 13-year old sees her father beat her mother.

Many men act as if they are on the prowl, but as soon as it looks as if they are capturing their prey, they flee in the opposite direction. Chalk this and other male hang-ups to early fears of impotency or castration. Often the sexual responses of men—such as ejaculating too soon, or not at all—can be traced to non-sexual experiences that now are being expressed sexually.

Vital Steps for H-C Programming for Sex

Step One: identify the hang-up. Use your pendulum to track down its cause. Nullify the cause by using the following H-C reprogramming:

> I am ready to drop this (behavior pattern). I no longer need it. I am free to be myself sexually. It opens up new levels of sexual enjoyment for me and my sexual partner.

Step Two in being yourself is to program you for uninhibited experimentation.

See yourself doing anything with your partner that you have the urge to do. No "what will he (or she) think of me" attitudes. See the sky as the limit in touching, caressing, kissing. Find new erotic zones in your partner. Try new sexual positions.

Take positions. Actually see yourself in different sexual positions. See her on top of you for a change, in a straddling position, or crouching on hands and knees. See yourselves side by side, her facing you or back to you. Change the position of the legs, or bend the knees or straighten them. See him on top of you; but now you have stretched your legs further apart, or one knee is up, or both knees are up, or you are part on the bed and part off.

This is not meant to be a manual on sexual techniques, but some readers need visual help in breaking out of set patterns and understanding in what directions experimentation and sexual adventure can go.

Once you feel you can visualize experimenting in bed, get into your H-C relaxed position and program yourself for greater sexual enjoyment.

Use H-C to Intensify Pleasurable Feeling

A divorcee reported to the authors that she felt no sensation in the sexual act. She had married at the age of 19, enjoyed a few years of normal, pleasurable sex with her husband, but the feeling began to wear off in her genitals. They became desensitized. Her husband sought his pleasure with other women and their marriage was on the rocks.

Now that she had her freedom, she still felt nothing with other men. A gynecologist had prescribed hormones but they had no effect. Now she was interested in H-C, and this is how it went.

She was asked to relax and concentrate on her left hand.

"Do you feel anything?"

After a moment, she replied, "I don't feel anything."

"Keep concentrating on the hand, and report any feeling."

After a few minutes, she said, "It feels heavier. And sort of warmer. My little finger just moved."

She was beginning to get "nerve messages." She was asked to give herself the suggestion that the next time these sensations would be stronger.

At the next sitting, she intensified these feelings. She was then asked to feel a warm blanket over her left hand, then a sensation of warm water flowing over it, then a sensation of warm air blowing on it. The sensations were quite effective. She could create a feeling of numbness in her right hand and compare this numbness with the heightened sensitivity in her left hand. Now she was ready to confront the problem.

At the third sitting, she developed a high sensitivity again in her left hand. She was then asked to transfer this to her vaginal area by touching herself and visualizing the sensitivity transferring to the clitoris and vulva. She used her visual imagination now to feel the warmth and sensitivity where they really counted.

After her first sexual encounter thereafter, she reported that she had felt a "new awakening" of her sexuality. She derived new pleasure from sex and had an appetite for it. The bitterness she had in her face when we first saw her had disappeared. She had a new softness and femininity in her face. Several months later she was engaged to be married.

Men or women can use H-C either to create more sensitivity or less sensitivity

Men who reach climax too fast, such as almost immediately after entry, as is often the case, can follow the same procedure as this woman, except they must create a numbness in their hand using imaginary ice water. This numbness is then transferred to the penis as follows;

> As I touch my penis with my numb hand, the numbness leaves my hand which returns to normal. It passes to my penis. I will feel all the pleasant sensations of sexual contact but not as sharply or intensely.

Experimentation is possible because either the extra sensitivity or numbness can be removed by going into your H-C state and visualizing or stating, "The feeling in my (vagina) (penis) is now returned to normal."

Should additional sensitivity be desirable, the process can be repeated several times. The sexual organs will not respond to any greater degree than does the hand. So the trick is to get the hand to respond better to your "warm" instructions. Give your mental computer the instructions that "next time the feelings of sensitivity will be more pronounced."

Orgasm: No Woman Need Be Without It

Mrs. R.L., age 26, had been married for five years when she came to the authors for help in her sexual dilemma. She had achieved orgasm with her husband before marriage and for a year after marriage.

Now she felt that life was passing her by. She feared she would lose her husband because of her lack of involvement in their sexual enjoyment.

Unlike the divorcee mentioned in the previous case history, Mrs. R.L, had not lost feeling in her sexual organs. She lost only the ability to reach a peak of excitement culminating in the involuntary spasms of sensory delight we call orgasm.

Discussing the situation with Mrs. R.L., we observed that she had feelings of resentment towards her husband originating from social and family matters.

What, in the reader's opinion, should be the first H-C reprogramming?

Correct. She gave herself instructions that she would express her resentments freely whenever they were felt. She would not keep them inside her. To augment this, she also gave herself ego-strengthening images.

The next H-C reprogramming was designed to reinstate the orgasm, now that its blocks were being removed. This she did by visualizing how she felt several years ago having an orgasm with her husband. She instructed herself to visualize how relaxed and calm she was, how devoid she was of any resentment or anxiety, and how totally successful the coital experience was.

She reported back to us after three successful orgasms, and then we heard no more.

The most important programming that you the female reader can give yourself to help orgasm is *relaxation*.

Tension and anxiety are orgasm blocks. They are also the easiest problems to cope with by using H-C.

In numerous instances, H-C has been successfully used without actual programming instructions. In other words, the mere act of getting into a deeply relaxed state via finger levitation and countdown, shortly before sexual relations, proved rewarding.

Every woman, even those with hysterectomies, can have an orgasm.

If this is the problem, you now have available to you four avenues.

1. Remove antagonism or resentment by expressing it and conditioning yourself with H-C to feel it no longer.

2. Use H-C to experience in your visualizing the enjoyable experiences you can remember. See them happening again.

3. Use H-C to enhance feelings of sensitivity if needed.

4. Program yourself before the sex act to be totally relaxed.

Erection: No Man Need Be Without It

A mild-looking man in his thirties could get an erection only if he play-acted that he was a soldier breaking into a house, ordering the women to undress as men of the household looked on in horror, and then forcing a woman to submit to him sexually under threat.

Using this as a mental fantasy was often not enough. He had to back it up with some histrionics and even stage props. Needless to say, it interfered with many a partner's sexual cooperation.

Many years of psychotherapy failed to remove this. H-C did it in three sessions.

During the first session, he was asked to go through this little drama. He did so and got an erection. He was then asked to go through it again, stopping to give each mental step a number. When he breaks into the house, that is step number one. When he confronts the men and women with a machine gun, that is number two, and so on.

During the second session, he repeated the numbers slowly without imagining or fantasizing. When he got to number four (she takes her clothes off), he got an erection.

The third session was a reinforcing session.

He was then instructed to concentrate on the numbers at his next sexual encounter instead of on the circumstances. Intercourse "by the numbers" proved to be an unqualified success.

Once a man fails to perform in sex, he has planted the seeds for continuing failure. Anxiety is a sex depressant. He is also conditioning himself--programming himself--for failure by worrying about failure.

You can reprogram yourself for success and "undercut" the negative programming "by the numbers." Here is how:

Visualize the last successful sexual encounter in every remember-able detail. Now go over it again in the H-C state, giving each step numbers. Reinforce it with another session or two, repeating the same procedure.

You are now ready to apply the numbers to your next sexual encounter. Time them for erection at the appropriate time.

Congratulations!

Sexual Power through Love Power

The sex act seems to be replacing the love act.

Books, magazines, movies—all depict raw sex more and more, romance less and less.

Love in any man-woman relationship can add a new dimension to sexual pleasure, a dimension that transcends the limited sensual experience.

We can restore and reinforce love in husband-wife relationships by a two-step H-C exercise:

Step One. Write down all of your mate's assets on one sheet of paper, liabilities on another. Hold the liability sheet on your left knee, asset sheet on your right knee.

Step Two. Do your H-C relaxation. Then program yourself to ignore the liabilities by crumpling that sheet and dropping it to the floor. Program yourself to concentrate on the assets by reviewing these assets again in your mind. End your session, but keep the two lists for future reinforcing sessions.

Why not do it now?

H-C affirmations for love power

General H-C affirmations that "let love in" are:

> I receive as much love as I give.

> I am not afraid to love. Should it end, I will not be hurt. Instead, I will be enriched by the experience and be able to love on an even higher plane thereafter.

> As I grow in self-worth and self-esteem, I am better able to love and be loved.

Other reinforcing suggestions that permit sexual vigor to rise with the rising of love:

> Deep relaxation of H-C restores my energy and sexual vigor as it permits warm feelings of love to flow.

> Sexual intercourse is an enjoyable release for my basic physical needs as well as a stimulant to deep feelings of love and affection.

> The more sexual activity I enjoy, the more I can enjoy as love grows to foster, replenish, and intensify.

How to Get Results for Yourself from Chapter 12 Now

Read all you can about sexual anatomy and techniques. Dispel ignorance. Next, dispel inhibitions, guilts and fears about sex, using the H-C reconditioning exercises provided. Advance your level of sexual sensitivity if needed. Program yourself through H-C for adequate sexual performance. Put power in sex with love.

13 – HOW TO TRANSFORM YOURSELF INTO A SUPERCHARGED IDEA GENERATOR AND PROBLEM SOLVER

What to Expect in This Chapter

Thinking is effortless with H-C power. No scratching of heads or furrowing of brows. You just turn on your "computer" and out come inspirational ideas, new inventions, and solutions to problems big and small.

The human brain radiates energy. This energy can be measured. Our brain actually oscillates in characteristic rhythms.

In our normal conscious state, this rhythm runs some 14 to 21 cycles per second. This is the active living rhythm when we are using our senses of sight, sound, touch, smell, and taste.

When we get into a relaxed state mentally, this brain wave rhythm drops from 14 down to 7 cycles per second. This is the rhythm that is characteristic of meditative and pensive states. Instead of being attuned to the outer world, we experience a type of inner consciousness.

Below 7, and down to 4 cycles, is the sleep state. However, the sleep state is not confined to this area as, during periods of rapid eye movement when dreaming is occurring, the brain waves can move up to 10 and 12 cycles per second.

Psychologists and others working with brain waves and their connection with behavior have given Greek letter designations to these various states as follows:

State	Cycles per Second	Designation
Outer conscious	14 - 21	Beta
Inner conscious	7 -14	Alpha
Sleep	4 - 7	Theta
Unconscious	Below 4	Delta

Solving problems and generating ideas take place best in the alpha state.

This is the state you are in when you relax and get a finger levitation. It is the H-C state.

The Alpha Level of Brain Activity Holds the Answers

The Rand Corporation is often called the "think tank" of America. Its clients go to them to generate ideas and solve problems. Rand offices are quiet places. Their personnel enjoy a relaxed atmosphere where the senses of sight and sound are not intruded upon. They seek an alpha level for best inner conscious thinking.

The alpha level is reached by quiet meditation. It can also be reached by hypnotic techniques such as those you use in reaching an H-C state. It is the same state that those who practice yoga seek to reach.

Exciting things happen in the alpha or H-C level:

- Your memory improves.

- You concentrate better.

- You recall at will.

- You develop your intuitive sense.

- You increase the flow of "inspired" ideas.

- You activate your creative imagination.

How an architect used H-C power

An architect who was still a junior in the firm was asked to come up with a proposed redesign of an existing resort area in the Caribbean. It was part of a competition that the firm was anxious to win. It decided to draw on the creative talents of every staff member.

A great opportunity? A chance for this young architect to exhibit his talent for design to his senior colleagues? Possibly, even to have his design entered by the firm? Even win the competition?

No. He felt none of this. "If they would only tell me what they want, I'd produce it for them," he complained to us. "Put who do they think I am to come up with such a solution single-handed."

Who, indeed! We discussed his training at the university from which he received his architectural degree. Yes, he had to carry out such design projects. Yes, he earned commendations and was on the dean's honor list when he graduated.

Why then did he feel he was not creative? Why was it that he felt he could only do what he was told to do? Why could he not produce an original design?

"I can only copy other people's work. I am best at working on mechanical details. Design problem solving is not my 'thing'..."

His protestations came slower and slower.

You could tell it was getting harder and harder for him to believe what he was saying.

He was venting or releasing those feelings of self-limitation. The negativity was being dispelled.

Then came the switch.

"Wait a minute," he said. "I'm beginning to think there's something wrong with what I'm saying."

"Try the opposite on for size," we suggested.

"I *am* creative. I do know how to design creatively."

We had him program himself in a deep H-C state with that statement. Then, when he ended his session, we had him make the statement aloud again.

It came out easily.

He believed it.

He knew it.

He couldn't wait to get back to the drawing board. Instead of spending hours "sweating" over the project, he now fell all over himself trying to delineate his ideas as fast as they came to him. As he described it later, "All I had to do was follow my pencil." He wound up with a design that became part of his firm's final presentation, which eventually won honorable mention in the competition.

Like any other activity, thinking requires a programming of "I can." If you are programmed by past failures or rejections to feel "I can't," you've got a problem. Brother, you just won't be able to, no matter how hard you try.

Program yourself with "I can" and watch yourself light up the sky.

Do it now. Get into your H-C position and, like the architect, program yourself out of old failures and into new successes:

> In my alpha level, I am creative. I get ideas. I solve problems. My intelligence can provide answers and solutions for any and all situations.

How to Have a Photographic Memory

by Means of a Raised Finger

Mr. N.E., a man in his late fifties, had his heart set on going into the Coast Guard now that he had retired from business. He took the exam five or six times, failing each time because of his apparent inability to concentrate, remember, and recall during the exam.

He was instructed to record the course material and play it back to himself while in the relaxed Hypno-Cybernetic state. This he did. He went on to pass the examination with the highest mark ever recorded by the Coast Guard.

For those who do not have recording capabilities, having others read to you while you are in the H-C state is, of course, just as effective.

Good H-C subjects can open their eyes and read without disturbing their alpha (relaxed) state. Program yourself first as follows:

> I am able to open my eyes and read with my finger in levitation. Reading will not disturb my relaxed state. Everything I read in this state, I will remember and be able to recall at will.

In Japan, the use of hypnotism in learning is used much more widely than in the United States. Even as early as in fourth grade, students are improving their memory, writing, and reading through a teacher's use of group hypnosis.

In this country, as early as 1934, W.H. Gray reported in the *Journal of Education Psychology* how hypnosis accelerated the learning of spelling. In 1955, International Morse Code was being taught more rapidly with hypnosis.

You have acquired in your H-C technique a magic wand for learning. Use it anytime you want quick, accurate results.

How professional performers benefit from H-C

Dr. William S. Kroger has used hypnotism to help a number

of motion picture, stage and television performers, who were having middle-age memory problems, to learn difficult roles quickly. First, inhibitory factors are de-programmed and positive attitudes reinforced, This is the same old story of self-limitation providing a stumbling block that must be removed.

Next, concentration is improved through suggestions that remove the distraction caused by external stimuli.

When the lines are then memorized, a final step is taken: the actor visualizes a rehearsal while in the equivalent of his H-C state and "hears" himself go through his part. He can do this a number of times in short order because time is distorted. A two-hour show can take as little as ten minutes.

With the above method, the lines can be memorized in the regular manner—and it goes faster because of the focused concentration—or the lines can be memorized in one extra sitting by their being read to the actor by another person while the actor is in his alpha, or hypnotized, state.

Summarizing this memory method for H-C use:

1. Program yourself for "I can."

2. Program yourself for concentration—"I am totally absorbed in what I am reading. Outside noises or influences do not distract me."

3. Program yourself with the material. Have it played back to you with a recorder or read to you.

4. Reinforce your memory by going over the learned material as your final H-C exercise.

A phenomenon with the impressive tag "hyperesthesia" is quite effective in aiding concentration. Hyperesthesia was used in the previous chapter to heighten tactile sensitivity. It can also be used to heighten sound, sight or smell. Of course, for book study we would use it to heighten sight. We would not use the warm water technique, but rather direct instructions.

Where general study is involved, the following H-C programming can be immensely helpful to the student. It assumes that negative factors that produce "I can't" programming have already been removed, and it uses hyperesthesia:

> My study is very intense to me. It fills my senses. Outside sounds are unimportant to me. I hear them less and less. I recognize only sounds of danger. My study is satisfying and attention filling.

Problem Solving with Your Mental Computer

Ten engineers were given a difficult design problem in an experiment to test the problem solving power of H-C. Five were instructed to proceed as they would ordinarily, without hypnotic techniques. Meanwhile, here is what the other five did.

They were told to familiarize themselves with all aspects of the problem by the usual study method. They were then told to enter their H-C state and program themselves to come up with the solution the following morning.

There was a mighty quick decision. The control group were still in their initial work when the H-C group were ready with their solution. The former were so outclassed they suspected collusion.

Bernard Baruch, the late millionaire park bench philosopher, advised presidents and cabinet members who consulted him to "sleep on it." He was saying, in effect, let your brain go to work on it while you're not standing in the way.

You can use the "sleep on it" method by getting a finger levitation and then programming yourself to have the answer the following morning:

> My problem is *(review the problem)*. I see myself with the answer when I awake in the morning.

Or you can get faster action by getting out of your mind's way by another means. When we are asleep, our conscious mind is not whirling and keeping out messages from the subconscious. So when we awake, that message is waiting for us. We can accomplish the same result by keeping our conscious mind from whirling.

It is not easy to keep your mind blank. The average person who tries to think of nothing finds himself thinking of something in from one to three seconds, even if it's just thinking about himself thinking about nothing.

However, by using a simple H-C technique you can quiet the mind for long periods. This is called passive concentration. You need to pick an object that acts as a "crystal ball." It can be imaginary or real. You can use a glass of water or a window shade pulled down.

Sit in your H-C position, eyes open, and stare at it, *expecting* the answer. You can use an imaginary body of water or screen just as effectively. You can even imagine a blue sky or a gray wall.

The answer can come immediately or in a few minutes or you might require another session in a few hours.

How to Turn Up the Power of Your Idea Generator

Many computers appear to do more than compute. They seem to be able to "create" original ideas. Since a computer is limited to producing only products of what has been programmed into it, originality would seem impossible.

Actually, what happens is this. A decision table is programmed into the computer. That is, a number of possible conclusions are fed into it based on a number of assumptions and premises. Then, what is known as Boolean logic is used to combine answers in many ways. The results can be some very exciting "discoveries."

The human mental computer can do this and much more.

However, the human computer has some blocks that need to be removed before it can hold a candle to its electronic "brother." These are the same "I can't" blocks that we have had to remove before. Only, in the case of creative thinking, it translates into:

"I am an amateur in this field." Or,

"I am an individual. How can I expect to succeed where groups of experts working together fail?"

Let's shoot down both of these right here and now.

Of course, professional inventors have been very successful. But the amateur approaches a problem with no limitations (if he can scratch the one about being an amateur). He doesn't eliminate possible answers, as the professional might, because they won't work. The amateur is too "dumb" to know this. He just goes ahead and does it. Like the sign purported to hang in the office of the president of an aeronautical firm that said in effect: a bumble bee's wingspread is so much; its dihedral angle is so much; its weight is so much. According to all the laws of aerodynamics, the bumble bee cannot fly. But the bumble bee does not know this.

An amateur can be just as good dredging up ideas for games as somebody who has come up with 20 successful games in the past. He can innovate more easily in any line of thinking than an old hand at that particular line of thinking.

Understand this. Agree with it. And you need no H-C exercise. The block is removed.

Second block. Stand back, this one's going to fall fast. Do you think that if it takes two days for one person to come up with an idea, two persons can come up with an idea twice as fast, say, one day?

Try it sometime. Two people get in each other's way. Perhaps they'll each take two days to come up with the same idea. Or perhaps they'll take two days to come up with different ideas and spend a week trying to choose between them.

Large labs come up with plenty of patents every year. But Edison worked largely as an individual at Menlo Park and you know what he developed. An exception? Well, here are some inventions by other "loners"–the helicopter, quick-freezing for foods, the self-winding watch, your car's automatic transmission, the zipper, and a number of medicines such as penicillin and streptomycin. In fact, more of the major inventions of this century have come from individuals than from large industrial research organizations.

Translate block number two into an H-C programming instead:

> As an individual, I have an advantage over research teams. I function as an idea source, complete and limitless.

High Voltage Thinking without Half Trying

With these two blocks out of the way, you are now able to proceed to turn up the power of your idea generator. You can use your automatic mind to solve problems as simple as tic-tac-toe or as complicated as designing a luxury liner.

Your mind can tell you what the best foods are for you to eat, what time to get up in order to be where you have to be, or which friend is the right one to go to borrow a lemon.

You also have the ability to turn your mind on to problems that you would appear to have no way of possibly knowing, and still getting remarkably accurate answers. More about this at the close of this chapter.

With H-C you do not teach your mind any new tricks. You just permit it and instruct it to proceed.

How does your mind proceed to generate ideas?

The most common process is known as association. The mind associates an old method or material used in the past with a new application to solve a present need.

Suppose you had to get rid of a large inventory of used brick as there was a building freeze on. You have decided against costly shipping to some other area. You must come up with new uses for brick.

You remember a heavy object being used as a paper weight. You associate the two. Perhaps the bricks can be spray painted to add decor and used for paper weights. This leads you to door stops. Spray painting leads you to artistic possibilities. How about taking it from here and seeing where associative thinking takes you?

When you hit a dead-end, go into your H-C state and see if more ideas come.

An offshoot of associative thinking is free association. This is where one idea follows on another with no apparent connection. You sit back and let it happen. Psychologists and psychiatrists often use this to get insights into patients' subconscious minds. Sometimes the flow that free association produces can be symbolic, other times it can be too literal.

Here is an example.

You would like to darken one side of a divided room but there are lights on in the other side and the partition goes only part way to the ceiling. You sit down with a pad and paper and start with the word "dark"

Dark... Night... Eerie... Black coffee ... Bright light... Bright coffee ... Black light.

Black light! Of course, you'll paint the bulbs in the lighted room black on the side you want dark.

If there was ever effortless thinking this is it.

Like associative thinking, free association works even better while you are in a deep state of relaxation. Your H-C state is perfect.

No programming necessary here. You don't have to program a computer to be a computer.

What you are doing by getting into your H-C alpha level is getting the limited conscious mind out of the way and permitting the vast circuits of the automatic mind to go into operation.

There are a number of thinking techniques that work well.

When a thinking technique works "well," it works "super well" when you use a light hypnotic or meditative state. Here are some more of these thinking techniques. Try them with and without H-C and see the difference.

Reference book technique. This is popular with inventors, writers, designers, artists and many others. You simply open the telephone book to the classified pages and look at all the job headings. It triggers ideas. Other idea-triggering reference books are tool catalogues, encyclopedias, dictionaries (including the quotation or rhyming kinds), business directories, "Who's Who," thesaurus, etc.

Brainstorming technique. This is a common technique in large firms where a number of people "free wheel" in their thinking in order to come up with a large quantity of ideas out of which they hopefully glean one or two good ones. Get somebody to join you on this as one person helps to trigger the other.

Check lists. This is in common usage and should sound familiar to you. Make a list of all aspects of the problem to be solved, or of the service or product to be improved, or of the avenues that can be explored in seeking a solution. The check list serves to direct the problem-solving attention of the mind to specifics, one at a time.

Visualization. You visualize the problem. If it is a question of shortage of storage space, see the clutter, see things in the way, see other aspects of the problem. Now see the solution taking place. Where is the clutter going? How are the aisles being cleared? This is made to order for H-C.

If you need to read or write or converse with others in order to carry out any of these techniques, you can remain in your H-C state for highest creative thinking effectiveness. You do this by giving your mental computer instructions as follows:

> I am deeply relaxed. I am in contact with my subconscious mind. I will now open my eyes and (read) (write) (talk) without ending this relaxed state. When I complete my project, I will end the session with the mental count 1-2-3 and I will feel fine.

In this alpha state, the brain often performs beyond the ability of science to explain. It can identify objects that cannot be seen. It can locate objects that have been lost.

Deep states of hypnosis permit regression beyond birth to what might be called "other lives."

The whole area of extra-sensory perception and extra-sensory projection, as some term the sending of consciousness to other dimensions beyond time and space limitations, responds to H-C in an unexplainable manner.

Suffice it to say that H-C permits you the full use of your magnificent brain.

And that instrument often performs beyond our conscious ability to explain.

Give it a try. Dream the impossible dream. Ask your mental computer how to get you there. Then watch it happen.

How to Get Results for Yourself from Chapter 13 Now

There is no problem you cannot solve, alone with your mental computer, no matter how new it appears. Give yourself the reinforcing instructions you need to know this. Also give yourself the "I am creative" programming. Now you are ready to improve your memory, learn more easily through better concentration, or develop ingenuity and inspiration. Go into your H-C state whenever you wish to connect your conscious "aware" mind with your resourceful subconscious. Be a brilliant problem-solver.

14 – HOW TO END FIDGETING AND NERVOUSNESS THAT ROB YOU OF SERENITY AND SUCCESS

What to Expect in This Chapter

"Relax." "Don't worry." Easy for somebody to tell us this, but just about impossible for us to do at times. Here come powerful mental techniques to program you for the most blissful, limp repose you have ever enjoyed. They will provide a flood of energy and confidence and put you in the driver's seat, calm and in control.

Mr. L.T. was a musician. He was a good enough singer to be able to pick up sufficient weekend club dates and tours for a living. His primary interest, however, was in composing music. He longed to see his work as a composer published.

The problem was he was anything but composed himself.

He had just been divorced. Prior to his marriage, and now, he experienced only short term relationships with women. Then they would break up. He had no friends, no social circle. He was jittery, unpleasant to others. He even appeared to dislike himself. That's why he came for help.

In his H-C state, he asked for the cause of his nervousness and sour disposition. He requested the answer within three hours. His answer came right on the stroke of the time limit: he felt deep inside that the music he was composing was not good enough and there was no use in attempting to push it.

The rest was easy. He reprogrammed himself for feelings of stronger ego. He could bear rejection by music publishers and/or women. He acquired a "you can't win them all" attitude. He was now able to circulate his music without taking rejections personally. At the present writing, he has not yet been published, but he has many friends, enjoys his vocal work more, and the girls keep arriving on his scene.

The case of Miss T.M.

Take Miss T.M., an assistant at a television studio. She was suffering the remorses of her fourth affair when she sought H-C relief. She had a penchant for married men. She seemed to punish herself by getting involved over and over again, despite her knowing it was only going to lead to heartbreak.

Now she was losing confidence in herself. She felt confused and at a loss to cope with her own emotions.

She used three H-C reprogrammings:

1. "I am in control of my emotions."

2. "I am a capable and attractive woman."

3. "This is a universe in which order prevails and in which I take my place.

The first two were obvious in their intent. The third was used to dispel confusion. However, the third had a happy side effect. It restored her respect for the marriage vows.

How to Pick Your Picture for Mental Repose

In each of the two cases just cited, an underlying problem caused nervousness and frazzled feelings. Even though there was no deep probing into the problem, substantial relief was attained by direct programming of needed reinforcement.

The same procedure is even more successful with less deeply rooted problems. For instance...

Suppose you are just plain jittery. Call it coffee nerves, or morning-after nerves, or whatever else you think it is. The important thing is you can knock it out and replace it with serene mental repose instantly with H-C

The way to do it

Here is how. Get into your H-C state as described in chapter 3. While in a relaxed state, pretend you are in a quiet, peaceful place that you know about. Picture this place. Feel the tranquility of it.

This peaceful place might be a grassy meadow. If so, you imagine you are there. You smell the fresh aroma of grass. You watch the fleecy clouds drift slowly by.

Your peaceful place might be a rowboat drifting on a quiet lake. You hear the water lapping and feel the gentle rocking.

Your peaceful place might be on a beach, or by a brook, or on an apartment house roof under the stars.

Pick a place that exists in your experience. This is a "must" because your visualizing must be "as if' it were true.

As you sit in your H-C session, visualizing this favorite peaceful spot, appreciate the calmness of it, enjoy the peaceful aspect of it, feel yourself being quieted and renewed by it.

You *will be* quieted and renewed. Even if you just sit in this reflective posture for only thirty seconds, you will feel as though you had a refreshing nap. Your nerves will be settled and you will have a distinct feeling of well-being.

But you will not want to interrupt such a peaceful moment.

Thirty seconds is too little time for bliss. Let it run for one, two, even three, minutes. Feel the calmness of nature. Soak it in.

Why not try such a session right now? You'll be glad you did.

Techniques for Quieting the Mind

My spot is a little rocky promontory that juts out into this stream. I sit there with a fishing pole and usually the fish don't bother me. But what does bother me are the thoughts about business. Will so-and-so call? Will my secretary take care of this and that?

His problem is a common one. The mind is programmed to run. And run it does. It runs over little details and then it runs over them again. We review what happened a few hours ago and what we want to happen a few hours hence.

The mind is not used to being quiet.

When we succeed in quieting it, nice things happen. It is as if our mind becomes a radio receiver instead of a radio transmitter. It receives whatever "station" we tune it to.

- If we quiet our mind and attune it to peace, we become peaceful.

- If we quiet our mind and attune it to energy, our exhaustion is relieved and our level of energy is replenished.

- If we quiet our mind and attune it to love, we become tolerant and loving.

So it pays to rout the thought gremlins that interfere with our quiet mind. If the peaceful scenes are not enough, here is what else you can do.

One effective technique is to visualize yourself in a light gray cloud. Thoughts cannot enter this cloud. They cannot penetrate through to you. You are surrounded by this thought protection, free to attune yourself to tranquility, energy or love.

For some, a cloud proves to be quite penetrable. They need to build a room around themselves. Make this an imaginary room with light gray walls, floor and ceiling. The walls are bare. The room is sound-proof and thought-proof.

Do not exert an effort to keep thoughts out. Exertion is the opposite of relaxation. It is not what we want. Instead, let the thoughts drift in one at a time if they insist. Watch them. Then let them drift out. Soon, with you watching them, they will get the message and you will find your mind quiet at last.

For stubborn cases, here is a useful technique. You are sitting in a quiet room. There is a blackboard in front of you. On it are the numbers 1 through 10. If a thought enters your mind to intrude on your passivity, you mentally arise and erase number 10. If it happens again, you "get up" and erase number 9, knowing that when you finally erase number 1, your mind will be a clean slate.

How to Be Cool, Calm, and a Winner in Sports

Nowhere are the effects of jitters and tension seen more vividly than on the playing fields, bowling lanes, tennis courts, and golf courses.

Your first step in H-C is to instill confidence. Your next step is to see yourself performing perfectly.

Champion golfer Gary Player believes you should be not just confident but overconfident. The average confident golfer might think to himself as he addresses his approach shot, "I'll chip the ball as close to the cup as I can and then hole out with one putt."

Player goes one giant confident step further. He visualizes himself sinking the ball on the chip shot. He often does exactly that.

A professional baseball player was hit in the head by a pitched ball while at bat. It knocked him out. The subsequent times he went to bat, he was tense. His stance changed. He seemed to be concentrating more on the ball hitting him than on hitting the ball. Of course, his batting average suffered drastically and he sought reprogramming.

Mental instructions for him were to be confident the accident he suffered was tremendously against the odds. It was not likely to happen again, especially considering his fast reflexes. He then "saw" himself standing up to the plate confidently, swinging energetically, and hitting line drives one after the other. He no longer suffered batting jitters after that, and his average went back up.

Confidence and perfection can be combined into one programming step by most players. The simple technique is to visualize yourself playing the game perfectly.

If you know the golf course you are to play on next, see yourself teeing off at the first hole. Then play the entire 18 holes in your mind's eye. Every drive, chip and putt is perfect, right up until the time you sink the last. Time is re-established in H-C so you'll take only three or four minutes for this kind of a practice session.

The Value of Practice Sessions

Two or three such practice sessions pay off even more than the real thing. Real practice has its negative programming as well as positive. You see the rough, the water hazard, the trap. You are programming yourself negatively. Real practice is much more productive if you see only the ball's perfect flight and arrival at its destination.

In tennis you see the perfect serve. Ace! Or the perfect passing shot or lob. Game for you.

In bowling, it pays to know how to play for a strike, or how to handle a two-one split. Then as you step up to bowl, you see the ball rolling to that exact spot.

If you have never seen the pins explode in a perfect strike, your subconscious image is incomplete. If you have never seen a line drive go over the left field wall, or a 30-foot putt drop into the cup, or a fast game of Ping-pong, your subconscious needs to be educated in those games if it is to provide you with the skills you need.

You can take your first step along the championship road right now by viewing films, photos, or actual play of the game in which you wish to excel. Watch some good players in action.

As soon as a drive has been completed, close your eyes and picture what you have just seen. The stance, the grip, the practice swing, then the real swing, the impact, the long straight flight of the ball.

In bowling, be able to "play back" the image the same way. Watch a 220-bowler hook the ball right into that one-three pocket. Then close your eyes and visualize the approach, the backswing and the delivery. Watch the ball in your mind's eye as it makes the hook and hits just to the side of the head pin.

How to end tension and jitters in sports

Tension and jitters play havoc with athletic prowess. H-C ends all types of jitters and tensions–the kind that are produced by large audiences or large stakes, and the kind that are produced by the private life of the individual player.

Get a finger levitation. Deepen your relaxation. Quiet your mind with a passive scene. "Drink in" the tranquility. See yourself winning at the game, making all the perfect shots.

Ready?

One woman improved her bowling so radically and suddenly through the use of H-C that she was ready to drop her job as fifth grade teacher and turn pro. One week, she was average in her league. The next, she was offered a job by the lanes running a woman's bowling clinic. "The only reason I did not take it was I really had nothing to teach except Hypno-Cybernetics."

They already knew they had to get the ball in the 1-3 pocket. They already knew the stance, the placement of feet, the steps to the foul line, the straight arm delivery, the release. They would not be absolutely green to the game.

All she could really teach them that they did not know already was a mental technique that would automatically ensure their concentration on the target; another mental technique that would give them the knowledge that they could produce that strike or a spare; and a third mental technique that would rid them of muscle-inhibiting tension and make them thoroughly relaxed.

There was more to teach in fifth grade.

Yet there are some H-C tricks you can use to increase your skill.

While visualizing yourself making a putt, exaggerate the size of the hole. See it so large you just cannot possibly miss.

While visualizing yourself pitching, see the plate larger, or batting, see the ball larger.

While visualizing yourself bowling strike after strike, see the pins larger.

Everything becomes easier, meaning your skill becomes greater as your mind programs your movements faultlessly.

H-C to Lighten Burdens and Lessen Anxieties

Leaving his office one day, Mr. R.L. suddenly experienced such pounding of his heart he was convinced he was having a heart attack and would die.

Medical examination disclosed nothing wrong with his heart. Still, these "attacks" continued. They made him afraid to be with people, afraid it might happen on a bus or driving in a car. Just the idea of going to work almost paralyzed him with fear and anxiety.

During his first H-C session, his subconscious mind fed him the cause of his acute anxiety. A woman he was having an affair with, prior to the first attack, had been pushing for marriage. He rejected this as he did not feel capable of being involved with her on a formal basis. The anxiety attack was a subconscious device. It had given him an "out." He could blame his health.

No reprogramming was used, only simple periods of relaxation. He visualized passive scenes and used a number of count-down procedures to deepen his H-C state.

Advanced H-C Techniques

Here are several deepening techniques, in addition to the ten-to-one technique given you in chapter 11.

1. Concentrate on your breathing. Every time you exhale, see yourself sinking deeper and deeper into total blissful repose.

2. See yourself in a mine elevator shaft. There are ten levels. Count backward from ten to one as you descend. Know that when you reach the lowest level you will be so relaxed you will be on the verge of sleep.

3. Take three deep breaths. Know at the third exhalation you will go deeper than you have ever been.

4. Imagine you are taking a walk in a garden and stop to smell the fragrance of a particularly attractive blossom. There is a drop of water on one of the petals and it reflects the sun in many colors of the rainbow. You are transfixed by the many colors in this drop of water.

5. Use a metronome, grandfather clock, or any other clock or device that ticks loudly. Know that every tick takes you deeper and deeper into a limp state of body and mind.

Anxiety wreaks havoc in health and personal effectiveness.

Relaxation creates equal and opposite miracles.

Use H-C relaxation, the deepest most blissful you can attain, to conquer fidgeting, anxiety, tenseness, jitters and nervousness of any kind.

The relaxation programming alone may do the trick. No other specific programming may be necessary. Step up the frequency of your H-C sessions to obtain even greater calming effects.

Tailoring H-C Programming to Untie Your Knots

Dr. S.F., a 39-year-old physician, was always behind on his bills. For a good doctor, his income was exceptionally low, in considerable contrast to other doctors in the area.

He used the pendulum technique to discover any psychological cause for his low income professional pattern. The pendulum led him back to his parents' divorce. His father had complained bitterly that his wife had stuck with him during his lean years only to hit him with a fat alimony once he had achieved financial success.

Now, Dr. S.F. was applying this same fear to his own marriage. He was subconsciously afraid that if he was successful, his wife would seek a large property settlement and leave him.

Dr. S.F. then used H-C programming to enhance his own feeling of self-worth and his sense of security in holding on to the affection of his wife. He reviewed his success in treating patients. He relived the romantic moments he and his wife enjoyed.

Merely understanding what he was doing to himself would have helped. But the reinforcement of H-C programming paid off with a sharp increase in his office income.

Everybody's problems are different. Although the same principals are involved in solving them, the H-C programming must be tailored to fit.

Two Cases of Stuttering Healed

Take Mr. R.T. who had aspirations to become a singer in the entertainment field. He was a cantor by profession, who worked in synagogues in the Los Angeles area. His religious chanting and singing was marred by a serious handicap—he stuttered.

Since his stuttering was seldom evident when he talked, but present only when he sang, his H-C reprogramming involved seeing himself a perfect speaker, free of any stuttering whatsoever. In these exercises, he was not to consider himself a singer.

The desire to be a singer was obviously causing the anxiety that created the stuttering. Mr. R.T. was reminded that he did not *have to* become a full-time singer and cantor, that he was still young enough to go in a number of other professional directions.

This idea of there being a choice took away the anxiety. He no longer felt trapped. His singing improved. The stuttering receded. Eventually, however, he chose a different career.

By contrast, a woman who had once enjoyed a fine career as a concert singer came to the office suffering from what the specialists called "spastic disphonia." She could not speak or sing without stammering. The condition had started right after a tooth extraction. Despite her inquiries at various medical associations and physicians' offices, it took her 11 years of this career-interrupting stammering to discover hypnosis. But it took only ten H-C sessions to program out her fear and restore her ego. Her beautiful voice was restored in the bargain.

Why do people permit themselves to suffer when relief is so close?

The longer tension and anxiety persist, the greater their destruction in terms of health and success.

There is another possible side effect that might have to be reckoned with.

A recent study reported in *Science* shows that uncontrolled hypertension can cause significant impairment to the intelligence. Drs. Frances Wilkie and Carl Eisdorfer, working at the Duke University Medical Center in Durham, N.C., observed some 80 volunteers over a period of ten years. Those without high blood pressure continued to respond at their level to psychological testing. Those with high blood pressure and hypertension showed marked intellectual loss on the tests during the ten-year period.

How to Handle Jobs Having Built-in Hypertension

Some jobs have built-in hypertension.

A recent study of air traffic controllers disclosed that they have a higher incidence of peptic ulcers than any other known group.

Their fear of causing a mid-air collision produced ulcer symptoms in 86 of the 111 controllers involved in the study. One controller estimated he was involved in at least 50 near-collisions in a two-year period. Symptoms that accompany the stress in this job include insomnia, shortness of breath, and anxiety, as well as marital discord and interpersonal animosities.

If you are an air traffic controller, you have our condolences.

All the rest of you resolve here and now that any anxiety or tension you experience in your job you are largely bringing to your job yourself.

The choice is yours. You can be up-tight or play it cool.

You can dwell on the problems or on the solutions.

You can see the dark side or the bright side.

If you do tie yourself up in knots, untie them right now with tailor-made programming to fit the "crime."

Use relaxation techniques that deepen your H-C state.

Use natural scenes to pacify your mind.

Use direct mental pictures and clear-cut affirmations to build up self-image, self-worth, self-respect.

Then reprogram for what you need with simple "I am" statements:

- I am serene.
- I am confident.
- I am optimistic.
- I am secure about the future.
- I am calm.
- I am unperturbable.
- I am strong.
- I am in control.
- I am safe.
- I am happy.
- I am successful.

Add to these as you size up the need. Select. Combine.

Do it. The time you spend is tiny compared to the burdens you unload and the peace of mind you gain.

How to Get Results for Yourself from Chapter 14 Now

Get to know what a relaxed muscle is. Tense your jaw by biting down on your teeth—then let go. Do the same with your hands, then your feet. Tense. Let go. Pacify your mind and relax your body using the technique(s) that work best for you. Here's a useful device to save time: Before you end your session, program yourself to "go deeper and faster whenever I say 'relax now.'" Or substitute your own code word for "relax now." Program yourself for serenity and assuredness.

15 – HOW TO COPE WITH NAGGING HEALTH PROBLEMS THAT DRAIN YOUR YOUTHFUL VITALITY

What to Expect in This Chapter

Here are valuable H-C commands to:

- *End backache and headache*
- *Create temporary numbness to pain*
- *Alleviate skin conditions and remove warts and blemishes*
- *Get rid of allergies*
- *Remedy nausea and other stomach symptoms*
- *Restore normal bowel activity*
- *Aid wry neck*
- *Relieve colds and respiratory ailments*
- *Help you to be more comfortable, whenever serious illness strikes*

If you skipped the last chapter because you have not been plagued with tension, it will still pay you to return to the subtitle "How to Pick Your Picture for Mental Repose." It is necessary to learn these valuable mind-quieting techniques. They are needed in the reprogramming procedures for total health that you are about to learn in this chapter. Also, you will need to understand and utilize the five H-C deepening techniques described in chapter 14.

The Role of Your Mind in Illness

A man suffers partial paralysis of his right arm after a minor collision. It fails to respond to treatment. Medical conferences disclose that he had argued with his father about a certain matter the afternoon of the accident. The immobilized right arm made it impossible to carry out his father's wishes. Once this fact came out in the open and the disagreement was resolved, the arm quickly responded to therapy.

A woman develops chest pains that point to a possible heart problem. Yet, examination discloses nothing organically wrong. Psychological investigation reveals that she has a need for more attention from her husband.

The automatic mind runs the body. We don't have to breathe or beat our heart. It is done for us. It is done by that part of the subconscious mind programmed for efficient bodily functioning.

Yet, that part of the mind does not live in a world of its own. Its programming for health is involved with the rest of the mind. And the rest of the mind is often anything but "health-minded."

What Happened to Several Great Financiers

Back in 1923, a meeting of eight of the world's great financiers reportedly took place at the Edgewater Beach Hotel in Chicago. Present were a member of the President's Cabinet, the president of the largest utility company, the president of the New York Stock Exchange, the president of the largest steel company, the most active "bear" in Wall Street, the president of the largest gas company, the president of the Bank of International Settlements, and the head of a world monopoly.

Twenty-five years later, here's what had happened to these eight illustrious men:

- The member of the President's Cabinet, Albert Fall, was pardoned from prison, severely ill, so he could die at home.

- The utility president, Samuel Insull, succumbed to his illnesses and died penniless in a foreign country.

- Stock exchange prexy Richard Whitney served time in a penitentiary.

- Steel baron Charles Schwab had to borrow money to pay his doctors' bills.

- Wall Street "bear" Jesse Livermore died by suicide.

- Gas company president Howard Hopson became insane.

- The Bank of International Settlements president, Leon Fraser, died by suicide.

- World monopolist Ivan Krueger died by suicide.

The Value of a Healthy Mind for a Healthy Body

A man's mind and his body are closely connected. Wholesome and positive attitudes and emotions can support a high level of good health and well-being. Any other types of attitudes and emotions contribute to inadequate mental and physical health.

Medical science now recognizes that mental stress and distress can lower bodily resistance to infectious diseases as well as cause imbalances in the functioning of vital organs.

The result is a virtual compendium of illnesses and physical conditions for which we ourselves are to blame—illnesses such as:

Respiratory—common colds, hay fever, bronchitis, asthma, sinus trouble.

Neural—alcoholism, drug addiction, migraine headaches, spasms, blindness, deafness, hiccups.

Digestive—diarrhea, heartburn, nausea, ulcer, colitis, constipation, obesity, hemorrhoids, gastritis.

Also affected—heart, liver, kidneys, blood, gallbladder, bones, skin, hair, nails.

Mental stress and anxiety cause all this, and they cause more. They interfere with automatic programming that we have taken for granted to be perfect.

We learn to ride a bicycle, drive a car, or fly a plane. We do not do it very well at first, but finally, with practice (programming) we are bicycle riders, licensed automobile drivers, or pilots.

If the programming would stop there, all would be well. But it doesn't.

Half of all auto accidents, according to leading insurance authorities, take place when emotional disturbances are present.

Attitudes of pilots, such as those brought on by arguments at home, have been the cause of plane accidents, says the Civil Aeronautics Board.

Long after we learn how to ride a bicycle, drive a car, or fly a plane, we continue to program our body with unwanted data that our body continues to respond to perfectly.

This is data that provides imperfect answers. It calls for wrong reactions. It puts a measure of anger into the accelerator, a touch of resentment into the steering wheel, and an assortment of emotional cacophony as a deterrent to safe travel.

Hypno-Cybernetics for good health and accident-free living

means programming for wholesome, positive attitudes and emotions.

It also means picturing perfect health and flawless bodily functioning.

How to Be the Picture of Perfect Health

If you can hold in your mind the picture of yourself in perfect health, you become that picture.

This may sound like Christian Science. But it also sounds like practically every other modality of spiritual healing through the ages.

Sounds easy, doesn't it? There's just one hitch: try thinking of your perfect head when its throbbing like mad. Or try visualizing yourself in brimming good health, when you're so nauseous you can't hold down a teaspoon of water.

It becomes a lot easier with H-C.

You relax. You get a finger levitation (it's best to be practiced at this rather than be trying it for the first time when in pain). You see yourself feeling fine. You see the particular problem gone.

Most of us program ourselves in just the opposite direction.

We dwell on the problem. Pain keeps calling our attention to the imperfect organ or body part. In fact, we can hardly take our mind off it.

With H-C your subconscious mind helps you to switch from problem programming to solution programming.

Relaxation softens pain. The H-C process is fast-in, picture, out. Enough picturing and the solution-better health-begins to manifest.

H-C for Temporary Relief of Pain

In chapter 12, the technique for adding sensitivity to body parts was described. The same technique, with some changes, is used to create numbness to pain.

Here's what you do:

1. You get into your H-C state.

2. You imagine that Novocain or another pain-deadening agent has been injected into your hand. Or, if you have never experienced something like this, imagine your hand immersed in ice water.

3. You test for numbness by pinching one hand, then the other.

4. When numb, you touch the painful part of your body with that hand and instruct the numbness to pass to that part.

5. You restore feeling to your hand by saying "my hand is now normal."

6. You restore feeling to the numbed part when desired by saying "my _____ is now normal."

Pain is nature's way of reminding us that all is not well. We should respect pain by seeking medical advice should it persist.

Under no conditions, use this H-C pain deadening technique as a continuing method of relief.

Use it whenever emergency or temporary relief is needed until you can see your doctor.

What to Do about Illnesses Which Do Not Respond Readily to Positive Mental Programming

If illness does not respond readily to medical treatment, chances are there are emotional causes present.

If illness does not respond readily to simple mental treatment —such as perfect health picturing—then the disease is organic (physical work). You must defuse the emotional cause before you can expect results.

There are clues to the nature of these illness causing emotions in the very diseases they cause.

You've heard such expressions as "Oh, my aching back!", or "He gives me a pain in the neck."

There is much truth in these popular sayings. That's undoubtedly how they came about.

Some situations that "gall" us actually irritate our gallbladder. "Heartbreak" can cause heart problems.

Psychosomatic medical files are still thin, but here are some of the clues turned up by repetitive case histories:

- Guilt, self-criticism, self-condemnation often lead to disorders of the lower intestinal tract and colon.

- Feelings of tension and pressure or of disappointment and depression can lead to heart trouble.

- Anger, resentment, hate affect the stomach, liver and throat most frequently. They are also a common cause of the common cold.

We can use our pendulum to identify the emotion and the very situation that is causing that emotion as described in chapter 9.

It may also pop into our mind if we ask for these answers while in an H-C session.

Once identified, relived, and re-evaluated, it may melt away.

Or else, you may require reprogramming such as:

I no longer feel hate toward _____. I rise above that situation. I am able to live and let live.

Dissipate these gnawing emotions and you get much better results from positive reprogramming for good health.

How Corrective Programming Works

Some years ago, Dr. Henry K. Silver, then professor of pediatrics at the University of Colorado School of Medicine, reported at a seminar on his research with dwarfed children. He found that these children suffered stunted growth when deprived of parental love, particularly mother love. Once that love is supplied, the children spurt upward, often catching up to others of their own age.

Research is still going on. What is the connection between love and bone growth? The child appears to grow normally for the first year, but eats twice as much as a normal child. After that, growth slows. The child continues to eat double the quantity, but bone calcification does not take place as fast as it should.

Place love in this picture and bone calcification speeds up while eating slows down.

The child's subconscious is doing what it can to make up for the lack of love and its effect on the bones by producing more hunger and therefore more bone material. But if love is the catalyst needed to make bones, no amount of programming or synthesizing of a feeling of love will take its place.

H-C is limited to the extent that it cannot supply what is missing.

It cannot reprogram you for health if you are suffering from malnutrition.

It cannot reprogram you for sight if your eyes are without functioning retinas or lenses.

It cannot, of course, in the case of leg amputation, grow you another leg. But it can eliminate the shock of the amputation, provide pain relief and prevent post-operative phantom limb discomfort.

Here is what H-C can do.

It can remove emotional causes.

It can reduce pain and discomfort.

It can accelerate healing.

It can reinforce healthy states.

There is a small pill that doctors use that has cured practically everything. The doctor writes out a prescription for it. The pharmacist fills the prescription. The patient takes the pill. The ailment disappears.

The pill is called a placebo. It is nothing but sugar, but the patient doesn't know this. "It is a medicine. And medicines work."

The active ingredients of the placebo are confidence, belief, and expectation.

If the patient knew he was taking a sugar pill, all bets would be off. It would knock the props out from under confidence, belief, and expectation.

These three ingredients are quite active in H-C reprogramming as well. All mental instructions must be given with *confidence, belief,* and *expectation.* You get back only what you put into it.

Don't sell H-C short because it requires these three "companions." So do many drug therapies. So-called miracle drugs owe some of their success to their dramatic arrival on the healing scene. Often, when the results of this initial public relations wear off, so do the drugs. This is then attributed to the body's building a tolerance or resistance to the drugs.

The power of suggestion is strong. It is strong because it is not suggesting anything. Instead, it is commanding.

H-C practitioners know that suggestions are in reality orders. These orders must be obeyed by a mental robot called the automatic mind.

How to Use H-C for the Common Cold

"Don't sit in that draft. You'll catch cold."

"Don't get your feet wet. You'll catch cold."

Maternal, protective, warnings? Yes. But they are also commands to the automatic mind.

Who knows how many noses run their course in the United States today because of those well-meant admonitions of a generation ago?

Another lulu: "Don't go near Johnny or you'll catch his cold." Years later, a nearby sneeze or cough can still be faithfully producing cold symptoms in the viewer.

Most colds are the faithful producing of symptoms by an obedient mind. It is like the hypnotized subject who is told a red-hot poker is being placed on his hand. Sure enough, a cool spoon produces a heat blister.

Colds are really caught when resistance to germs goes down. We all have cold germs in us constantly, but when our resistance is lowered, they take over.

What causes resistance to lower? It can be poor diet. But it can also be because he broke the date and she is taking it badly. Or, next week are the final exams.

H-C for preventing colds and respiratory ailments

> My resistance is high. I am not affected by negative suggestions and warnings about colds. I am resourceful and capable. Problems are challenges. I do not succumb – I overcome.

Other respiratory ailments respond readily to H-C reprogramming. Even though of emotional origin, this can usually be ignored in favor of direct symptom control.

Take asthma. This is usually associated with emotional dependency, coupled with extreme anxiety when that dependency is threatened. Yet when a junior-high school girl was given mental instructions that her attacks "would be less frequent and less intense," the response was dramatic. In her case, the attacks were preceded by coughing. The H-C instruction was also given to her that "you will cough from time to time without any asthmatic attack."

In two weeks, she was down to one mild attack per week. In two months, the asthma was gone.

Sinus, breathing difficulties, and nervous cough can also be helped with direct symptom control suggestions:

> I breathe easily.
>
> My windpipe and throat feel fine.

Allergies and Undesirable Skin Conditions

A young man of Japanese origin had large areas of skin on his back where there was no pigmentation. These white areas were raised slightly. They were on the increase. Dermatologists could not reverse the condition. He sought help through H-C.

Direct symptom control was used:

> My skin is perfect. It is uniform in color and texture.

Within one week the improvement was obvious. In one month, there was no evidence of the problem.

Skin conditions like warts and blemishes, undoubtedly caused by attitudes or emotions, respond beautifully to direct symptom removal commands:

> These warts will fall off. I see myself free of them.
>
> I do not need these blemishes. I am ridding myself of them. My skin is clear and attractive.

All types of allergies respond equally well.

If the material that appears to cause the reaction is known, the mental instructions may be directed at that material:

> Dog's hair is harmless to me. My nose is not affected by it. I breathe easily without difficulty of any type, whether exposed to it or not.

If the substance causing the allergic reaction is not known, that reaction can be dealt with directly:

> My eyes are comfortable. There is no smarting or excessive tearing.

> My eye muscles are relaxed and at ease under all normal conditions.

Relieve Backache, Headache, Even Wry Neck

The weight of responsibility can be felt in the back.

Anxieties too difficult to face can cause muscular spasms in the neck that twist it and turn the face away.

The pain of tension and pressure can be felt in the head.

H-C to relieve backache is two-pronged:

1. Responsibility is weightless. I handle it effortlessly. I am capable and confident.

2. My back is perfect. All bones and joints move in harmony.

Wry neck, known medically as torticollis, stubbornly resists physical therapy. Yet it responds miraculously to a two-sided H-C approach:

1. I can face life and its circumstances. I am insulated from irritation and anxiety. They do not touch me. I am resourceful, guiltless, and confident.

2. My neck muscles are relaxed. My neck moves freely and easily. It is normal in every way.

Headache can be relieved quickly by creating numbness in your hand and then transferring that numbness to the throbbing area of the head in accordance with instructions given early in this chapter. This is just a temporary measure. It should be followed by instructions that remove pressure and tension, custom-built to fit your situation or circumstances.

If time is the problem:

> I have all the time I need. Everything is working out in good time. I am comfortable about my rate of progress and accomplishment and that of others involved with me.

If indecision is the problem:

> I am confident in the outcome. As one door closes another opens. I am resourceful and optimistic.

Persistent migraine headaches may not respond satisfactorily to these mental instructions. However, here is a remarkable method that can be used for a number of similar stubborn problems, such as asthma, coughing attacks, and stomach spasms.

You go into your H-C state.

You instruct your mind to create a headache.

You imagine you have it.

You expect it.

You feel its beginning.

It arrives—actually.

You now reverse it.

You instruct your mind to remove it.

You imagine you no longer have it.

You expect it to leave.

It leaves.

You end your H-C session.

Now whenever a headache begins to be felt, you immediately return to your H-C session and take up at the "reverse it" point. It leaves.

One man, 26, had suffered for over a year when he tried this H-C method. It took him only five sessions to develop his ability to reverse any headache before it could get started.

How to Help Remove and Prevent Stomach Disorders

Worry and tension are prime suspects for many gastro-intestinal disorders. In fact, it was a stomach problem that provided a breakthrough for medical science's understanding of how emotions affect internal body chemistry. Decades ago, a man was operated on and in order to observe the results, doctors created a small window into his stomach. When the patient became angry or upset, doctors could observe the stomach turn crimson.

Stomach problems, from nausea to cramps to ulcer pains, can be helped by direct commands to the automatic mind to substitute relaxation for worry or excitement and to substitute a healthy stomach for the one you have:

> I will be calm and relaxed. I am free of worry. I do not get easily excited. I am serene and confident.

And then:

> My stomach problem lessens in frequency and intensity. My stomach is restored to a healthy state and operates normally, free of pain or discomfort. I feel fine.

For constipation:

> My bowels move easily and on schedule. No events or circumstances bother me so as to interfere with normal evacuation.

Supplementary instructions may be needed in the case of intestinal problems to motivate you to eat proper foods. Greasy or spicy foods can delay the recovery of irritated stomach linings. Sweets and starches, with no natural roughage, can delay the return of normal bowel movement.

> I no longer eat _____ which do not contribute to my good health. I feel it enjoyable and satisfying to eat the foods specified by my physician.

How to Get Results for Yourself from Chapter 15 Now

Help yourself to better health with the H-C instructions for specific ailments. Learn how to deepen your H-C state for greater effectiveness of your H-C commands. Give yourself this H-C command to maintain your good health at a higher level than ever before:

> Every day in every way my health gets better and better. I do not accept negative attitudes and emotions that detract from health. I am adaptable and changeable when necessary. I see myself in perfect health always radiating youth, vigor, and vitality.

16 – HOW TO REJECT DESPONDENCY, GRIEF AND DEPRESSION TO GAIN OPTIMISM, ENTHUSIASM AND YOUTHFUL DRIVE

What to Expect from This Chapter

Use H-C to dispel grief and gloom, to help you across difficult times, and to turn the cloudiest days into sunshine-flooded steps to a new life.

A woman was obsessed with the idea that she might be cancer-prone. She was listless and despondent. She became run-down and sickly. H-C efforts to see herself as a healthy, fit woman failed. She could not hold such a picture in her mind "as if it were true," because she knew it wasn't true.

H-C efforts were then turned directly toward the fear of cancer. However, this only seemed to intensify her anxiety.

The pendulum was then used to track down a cause. It was discovered that two or three times as a child she had come down with an illness just before a trip or a vacation. "Unless Nancy gets sick again" got to be a family byword.

Once this was reviewed in her mind and she saw the connection, she reacted perfectly to H-C reprogramming that she would feel composed and calm, that she had every reason to feel confident about her health, that she would be less apprehensive, feel more safe and secure.

Result: One woman able to enjoy life more.

The Truth about Grief

The loss of a dear one can be one of the most difficult periods in a person's life. The world seems so empty. Life seems so bleak.

Yet, turn the clock ahead a year. The grief is gone. New interests have filled the void. life is colorful again.

Actually, grief is a very selfish emotion. Selfless people seldom suffer from grief the way more egocentric people do.

Being selfish does not mean that we are any less of a person. We all have to be selfish to a degree to survive. But knowing that it is basically a selfish reaction, we are better able to handle grief.

Does an H-C approach for programming away grief come to mind? There are two pointed at in the paragraphs above:

1. My nerves are stronger and steadier. I am less preoccupied with myself. I see things in their true perspective.

2. I find new interests to replace old ones. I see myself independent, occupied and self-reliant.

Life can be bitter. Life can be sweet. The choice is ours.

Once we make the choice, we need to tell our automatic mind about it. Otherwise, it is still going to program us for feeling sorry for ourselves. We will continue to see life through gray-colored glasses.

We tell our automatic mind by getting into contact with it with our deep relaxation and finger levitation method. We communicate a message by visualizing it. "I see myself enjoying a sweet life."

The gray becomes rose.

The Way H-C Gives Us Control Over
Our Own Mood Cycles

The late Dr. Hornell Hart developed auto-conditioning at a Duke University research center where students kept records of their mood cycles.

Students would note when they had depressed or morbid periods and when these passed. Sometimes it took days.

However, when they used auto-conditioning—that is, relaxed and gave their receptive mind the right suggestions—they surged back to happy and lighthearted moods in as quickly as 18 minutes.

By using H-C the moment you feel down, you can prevent the entire down cycle. Do this a number of times and you can eliminate moods of depression altogether.

Here are the ingredients of mood changing H-C instructions. Put them together in any way that appears to counteract your own down mood the best. Use them at the first sign of gloom.

**Mood Table of Hypno-Cybernetic Instructions
That Turn "Downs" into "Ups"**

- Every day I become stronger and more courageous.
- I am less and less easily discouraged or depressed.
- My nerves are stronger and steadier.
- I am calmer and more composed.
- I am less preoccupied with myself.
- I feel cheerful and happy.
- I work with purpose and eagerness.
- I am no longer apprehensive or easily upset.
- I see things in their true perspective.

- I am mentally relaxed and confident.
- I enjoy life and feel optimistic about the future.
- I am pleased with each accomplishment.
- I know that my basic cheerfulness prevails and enhances my success.
- I appreciate the efforts of others and feel friendliness and rapport.
- I admire my own abilities and am confident in my own worth.
- I am free of guilt or self-contempt and feel only freedom and self-respect.

Select one, two, or three of the most desirable instructions to counteract your gloom. Feed them into your subconscious computer by repeating the words and at the same time seeing yourself as you describe.

Then feel the gloom turn to sunshine.

The One-Second Method to Dispel Gloom

There is a word that exists in every language. In French, It's "paix." The Russians say "mir." In Italian it's "pace," Spanish "paz," German "friede."

Of course, our word is "peace."

Over a quarter century ago, Joshua Leibman wrote *"Peace of Mind."* Overnight, it became a best seller and stayed on the bestseller list for an exceptionally long time.

Peace of mind is what most people long for. The popularity of the book reflected that yearning. If the book was republished today, it would probably turn in another impressive performance. Peace of mind does not go out of style.

There is one powerful H-C instruction that has been intentionally left out of the table. The reason is that it is extremely comprehensive. It covers any situation. You can use it instead of any of the instructions listed in the table. It is:

My mind is at peace.

In case after case of mood cycles, nervousness, and worry, a great relief has been attained with that "peace" instruction.

An accelerated H-C program method

Because it is so effective and so useful, a method has been devised to shorten the entire H-C process so that instant reinforcement can take place at the first sign of negative mood.

Here are the steps:

1. You do a regular H-C session, finger levitation, deepest possible relaxation, and then you give yourself the instruction, "My mind is at peace."

2. Before you end the session you instruct yourself that whenever you think the word "peace," it will activate and strengthen the "my mind is at peace" programming. Then you end the session.

3. Now, whenever a negative thought or emotion takes over, you think "peace." And it is dissipated.

4. Later, you can shorten "peace" to just the letter "p" by altering step two accordingly.

Once this method is mastered, then practiced, it provides instant relief for the agitated or the depressed. The quicker one remembers to use it, the better the results.

"I miss him so ... P... What a beautiful day."

How to Use a Mirror for Better Mood Control

When Emil Coue made famous the affirmation, "Everyday, in every way, I'm getting better and better," he asked that you look in a mirror while you said it. The mirror was used to strengthen the effect. That was close to the beginning of this century.

In 1948, Qaude M. Bristol wrote *The Magic of Believing* that sold over a million copies. He, too, advocated the use of the mirror to create better communications with the subconscious mind. He would have salesmen repeat into a mirror just what they wanted to sell to a particular customer before knocking on the door. And it worked.

Many great orators have used the mirror technique to enhance their magnetic projection, rehearsing before a mirror prior to important speeches.

Combining the use of the mirror with H-C programming is often a useful technique.

There are several ways you can manage this:

- Perform your H-C session in front of a full-length mirror. Open your eyes and look at yourself when you speak or image your mental instructions.

- Use a hand mirror in your chair. Keep your finger levitated as you use the other hand to hold the mirror, open your eyes and instruct yourself.

- Give yourself the instruction that you will remain deeply relaxed even though you arise and walk to a mirror. After looking in the mirror to give yourself mental instructions, return to your chair to end your session.

How to Transform Laziness and Apathy Into Energetic Enthusiasm

A man called the authors to see if his wife could be helped.

"She thinks life is just a bowl of cherries without the pits," he complained. "She never lifts a finger around the house."

"Does she work or have any hobbies?"

"She reads novels and screen magazines and watches TV. The only work she does is to go to bridge parties with her girl-friends." From the tone of his voice, the marriage wasn't doing too well.

"Does she want to be helped?"

"She agreed to my calling you and making an appointment."

It was arranged.

She arrived the next day on time. She was an attractive woman about 35, slightly overweight as might be assumed from her mode of living.

She complained bitterly that her husband expected her to do all sorts of work that she had never done before in her life. It appears that her mother always took care of the chores and told her to "enjoy life while she was still young."

"I understand your mother acts as babysitter for your two children a great deal of the time."

"Mother is a peach. Yes, she's a grand help."

"Is she also a grandmother to your children?"

She paused and seemed to tense up. It was as if this appointment and this office had been just another novel or TV show. Now, all of a sudden, it was real. Then came the second blow.

"Who plays wife to your husband?"

She felt like closing the book or changing the channel, but she was trapped. This was going to be no bowl of cherries.

Uses of Shock Therapy

Shock treatment is used for many depressed mental patients. A nurse presses metal plates against the temples. The current flows for a half second. The bolt convulses the patient and he loses consciousness. When he awakes he is greatly improved.

A psychologist was once taking part in a computerized program. The computer stopped working. The engineers could not budge it. The psychologist jokingly said, "It needs shock treatment." The engineers shot a bolt of current into the computer. It worked.

Life has its way of providing shocks when a person needs it. We do not advocate rough treatment. But the questions put to our non-wife, non-mother shook her up enough to realize that life was real, life was earnest.

She agreed to learn H-C on the spot. She was a good subject. She then gave herself instructions that she was a good wife to her husband, and a good mother to her children. "And I am getting better and better every day."

There was no overnight transformation. It took awhile. But she kept up the H-C instructions and gradually became enthusiastic about her marriage, her home, and her children—as if she found a new interest in life. When her husband paid the bill, he enclosed a one-word note:

"Wow!"

Just plain laziness is just plain goal-lessness.

Add a purpose or incentive to apathy and it can easily turn into enthusiasm.

Mr. K.W., 25, had dropped out of college after two years because he just did not care to study." Asked what he would like to do in life, he could not think of anything specific. He would like just to take each day as it came and do whatever suited him at the moment.

The reason K.W. came for help was that he had met a girl. She gave him an ultimatum. Shape up or ship out.

With H-C he reprogrammed himself to know that whatever

he undertook he could accomplish, and that accomplishment would bring him all he desired in life. ("Even Betty?" "Yes, even Betty.")

Then came specific instructions to go back to college and then seek work. This he did, getting a part-time job while he resumed his studies.

In an earlier chapter, we spoke about the difference between physical energy and life energy. In this chapter, we talk about the difference between no energy and life energy. Yet, the same factor is required to go from one to the other.

A goal, or plan, makes the difference.

And what a difference! Some people can go from the doldrums into a veritable cyclone of enthusiastic activity in a matter of days.

The H-C procedure is to:

1. Set a goal.

2. In H-C, see yourself moving toward that goal.

3. Reinforce with H-C ego-strengthening instructions.

4. Repeat with smaller H-C step-by-step instructions that make daily progress toward the goal.

5. Add the H-C instruction—"I am eager to reach my goal. I work toward it energetically and enthusiastically."

What to Do When You Are In Between Life Styles

Mrs. G.K., 45 and the widowed mother of four, found that with every passing month following her husband's death she became less and less concerned with her home and her children. As the clutter and dirt accumulated, she became reluctant to invite friends over and the children were embarrassed to have their friends visit.

One evening, the minister of her church visited unexpectedly. She was mortified. She decided she had to do something about her problem. She had read about H-C and resolved to try it.

Still in the process of deciding what kind of a life she wanted for herself, job or remarriage or neither, there was no possibility of well-oriented mental instructions.

The instructions that she did decide to use were aimed at:

1. Renewing her own self-esteem and self-confidence.

2. Seeing herself as she was before her husband's death and knowing that she could be that again—an efficient homemaker, a patient and understanding mother, and an attractive and vital woman.

3. Increasing her energy.

4. Keeping her problems in proper perspective.

Conditions improved at home. The children began to look more presentable and they became more cooperative. What the outcome was we don't know. But restored as she was to an effective woman, one has to believe that she is now enjoying a new phase of her life, whatever it may be.

A study was recently made in New York by Simmons College Professor Margaret Hennig. It was based on interviews with 125 top women corporation executives and was aimed at determining what made them "run." Were they really the aggressive types that no male would want to marry?

The results were remarkably close together. All had grown up with attachment to their father. Although they had a desire to marry and have kids, they put it off after college for a few years until they could establish themselves. The years stretched out to 12 and 15. Then something happened.

At about 35, they went through what you might call an identity crisis. They had to come to terms with the feminine side of their nature. Result: they dressed more attractively and even behaved more womanly. It did not interfere with their careers. If anything, it drove them further to the top. But everyone of the 125 then married, usually to an older man with children who was divorced or widowed. It was the beginning for them of a new lifestyle.

Everywhere, man is searching for identity.

He is reaching out of the colossus of the conglomerate, the morass of the megalopolis, and the growing sea of humanity for personal uniqueness and personal destiny.

For some men and women, it means loading the family in the car and driving away to the country.

For others, it means changing jobs, mates, or countries.

Still others just grow beards or throw away brassieres.

What they all are really doing is trying the doors of self-made prisons, built out of yesterday's values, and finding that the doors were never locked in the first place.

People are changing their lifestyles. They are "doing their thing." They are expressing themselves in new ways and broadening themselves with new experiences. They have a new awareness of life as a whole—where they have been and where they might be trying to go.

The hiatus between lifestyles can be painful. It is likely to be a period of discontent, soul-searching, and drifting.

Then something snaps and a new course is set.

Meanwhile, all you can do is give yourself the kind of H-C mental instructions that ease the growing pains and spur the decision to plot a new course:

> I have the freedom and desire to express my true self.
>
> I am confident in my resourcefulness and ability. I am self-reliant.

I have peace of mind now. I will be enthusiastic about a new course for my life when I set it.

How to Create a Burning Desire That Ignites Others to Help You

Once a goal is set, there can be no apathy, doldrums, or discontent. The plan has settled that.

However, there can be impatience, anxiety, and tenseness. What settles that?—Enthusiasm.

B.J. was a handsome 22-year-old fellow who never had trouble finding a job, despite his lack of a high-school diploma. But he had trouble holding a job. His good looks and dynamic personality gave him winning ways. The trouble was, if there was a chance to take a girl to the beach or for a drive in the country, he would just skip out. Result—a good time but no job.

Naturally, he could get enthusiastic about good times but not about good jobs. He could take them—and leave them.

His father told him about hypnosis and H-C training. He was intrigued. He relaxed quickly and deeply. His H-C reprogramming was directed at creating a new concept of jobs and of himself.

First, he used mental instructions directed at building up his own self-assurance. The fact that he did not have a high-school diploma did not mean that he always had to work as a run-of-the-mill flunky. He could be just as successful in a job as he was socially.

That was the bridge to instruction number two. Success in the job could bring him even more social success. It could bring him a sharp-looking car, admiration, more money for good times.

In a way, after the "ego" road was repaved, he transferred his social enthusiasm to job enthusiasm by equating one with the other.

Last we heard, he had been in a job for over six months and was moving up.

One of the most infectious human emotions is enthusiasm.

Analyze it, watch it in action, and its magic is elusive.

It appears to be just another hot emotion. But unlike anger, where the polarity is negative and the flame is red, enthusiasm has a purely positive polarity and the flame of emotion is white.

Enthusiasm is like the sun in its effect on people. It warms them and brightens their lives.

H-C for enthusiasm:

> I am turned on by *(plan, goal, activity, or job)*. I feel a burning desire, zeal, eagerness, and readiness. I move forward, winning the support of others through my geniality, goodwill and enthusiasm.

How to Get Results for Yourself From Chapter 16 Now

Conquer grief by understanding it and using H-C programming to combat it. Select the right H-C instruction from the mood table and turn your "downs" into "ups." Arm yourself with peace of mind programming that can be activated just by thinking the letter P. Harness enthusiasm to ignite the rocket that jets you to success.

17 – HOW TO ATTAIN AND MAINTAIN YOUR IDEAL WEIGHT WITHOUT WILLPOWER OR STARVATION DIETS THROUGH HYPNO-CYBERNETICS

What to Expect from This Chapter

Diets are out. A new way of effortless weight loss is available with H-C. Forget the carrot sticks and meals in a glass. Get ready for a thick steak smothered in mushrooms.

"If H-C can reprogram me to behave differently, can it make me eat differently?"

Thousands of now slender people roar an enthusiastic "YES!"

H-C works on weight control three ways. None of these ways entails starvation or willpower. Instead, plenty of delicious food. No effort.

Businessmen with large corporations who must eat and drink because their profits depend on it...

Women who gain during childbirth and never quite make it back to normal...

People with cravings for sweets or beer or ice cream or pastries...

Girls who aren't making it socially because they have a little too much here and there...

Fellows who find the extra weight creeping on and can't figure out why...

Models who need to take off only five pounds to get the top assignments...

Housewives who cook, attend fashion shows, teas and bridge parties, entertain, and eat and eat...

All have reaped the rewards of H-C's three-pronged attack on excess poundage:

1. H-C is used to identify attitudes and emotions that seek expression in eating and then neutralize them.

2. H-C is used to identify eating habits that are not the result of real hunger but of previous programming, and then replaces them with natural eating habits.

3. H-C is used to heighten desire for healthful non-fattening, high-nutrition foods and to erase desire for sweets, starches and other fattening, less nourishing foods.

These three steps can be accomplished as you read this chapter.

Of course, it is assumed that you have practiced the art of establishing communications with your subconscious (automatic) mind, according to the instructions in chapter 3. It will be helpful to you if, in addition, you have practiced some deepening technique to make your relaxation, and communicating, more effective.

Here goes then. Let's lose some weight the easy way.

How Early Programming May Still Be Moving Your Fork

In a way, everything that has been said in this book so far is working toward the success of this chapter.

When you set up a success pattern for richer daily living, chances are that you, like many overweight readers, are removing food as a substitute for that success pattern.

When you end money problems, eliminate fears and phobias, revitalize your sex life, chances are you are ending many more causes of overeating.

The same goes for frustrated leaders and executives, for people who are nervous and fidgety, and for those who have down moods and use food to give them a lift.

Why is food brought into the personality picture? What is the connection between frustration and apple pie?

"You were a good boy, Johnny. You can have a cookie."

"You straightened up your room very nicely Mary. When we go shopping, you can have an ice cream cone."

The words are long forgotten but the effects linger on.

We are programmed to consider food as a reward. The sweeter, the richer, the "icky-er," the more rewarding.

Infant thoughts of loneliness and insecurity are removed when the nipple comes into view. We become programmed to seek food when we need love or assurance.

Food becomes your medicine, your stimulant, your happiness, your security, your sex substitute—if you permit such programming.

You can tell those who have from those who haven't. By their bulk.

Recognize the pattern. Identify the attitude behind it. Reprogram yourself for a more positive attitude.

The case of Miss O.B. losing unwanted pounds

Miss O.B. weighed 230 pounds at the age of 29. It had been a vicious cycle. When she first went to work as a secretary, she was passed up for a promotion. She salved her wounded feelings with food and the scale moved up. More chances of promotion were missed. More periods of gustatory compensation.

Meanwhile, her skills were far excelling her modest office status. A senior officer, well aware of her outstanding ability, had a heart-to-heart talk with her about how her weight was standing in the way of her advancement. His own wife had benefited from hypnotherapy. He suggested some form of that if diets did not work.

When Miss O.B. discovered H-C, she had already tried all sorts of diets and taken all sorts of pills. The diets made her feel constantly hungry, tired, and listless. The pills made her mind foggy and her hands shaky. H-C was her last resort.

She was a good finger levitator. She attained a deep state of relaxation. First, she reprogrammed herself to realize her great abilities. Then she went to work on specific eating habits—those two portions of dessert she had at dinner, that second breakfast come office coffee time, and the box of chocolate in the lower left-hand drawer of her desk. She saw herself satisfied on three square meals per day.

Finally, she reprogrammed herself for steak, fish, and chicken instead of spaghetti, pizzas, and other starchy pastas. Salads and leafy vegetables were substituted for bread and potatoes. Fresh fruit replaced cake and pie.

In just a few months, she weighed 132 pounds. She looked years younger and immeasurably more attractive. Before the year was out she was holding a position worthy of her ability.

Are you willing to have a heart-to-heart talk with yourself? In the interests of heightened attractiveness, better health, and a longer life, are you willing to observe your emotions when the bell you call hunger is ringing? How do you feel at the moment of eating decision? What are you getting out of the food, besides weight?

How to Cooperate with Yourself

This is where you come in. You need to cooperate with yourself.

You need to have the motivation to take the mask off hunger and see just what emotional need is masquerading as the need for nourishment.

Use the pendulum if you need to. Or ask your automatic mind to deliver the answer to why you overeat, within three hours. (Be in a relaxed H-C state when you give the command.)

Once the attitude or emotion is identified, program yourself for its positive counterpart:

Insecurity: "I am a secure person. I have confidence in my ability."

Loneliness: "I am never alone in reality. I feel oneness instead of separation. I attract."

Anxiety: "I am relaxed, calm, and composed. I have assurance in myself and confidence in the future."

Frustration: "I feel warmth and understanding toward others. I do not anger easily. I am patient and in control."

Use positive approaches. Not: "I do not feel negative." Instead: "I feel positive."

Remember the affirmation in an early chapter? "Positive thinking brings me all the benefits that I desire!" This should set the theme for custom-built new programming that revises your emotional climate and sets the stage for a slimmer silhouette.

Anatomy of an Overeater

Her husband came home tired every night. Her hopes for love and affection disappeared at about 9:00 p.m. when he started snoring. And her trips to the kitchen began. About 10:00 p.m.— for a ham sandwich, some potato chips, a slice of coconut layer cake, and a glass of ginger ale. Later—she, too, retired.

She had a love affair going—with a refrigerator.

Some overweight people get up in the middle of the night for a snack. ("It helps me sleep better.")

Some take big portions and second portions and third portions.

Some skip breakfast, take a light lunch, then eat dinner from 5:00 p.m. to midnight.

Some have meals in between meals.

These are characteristics common to overweight people. Diet is not the answer.

When the diet is ended, the old habits return. And back up goes the weight.

Suppose you are in the habit of having a couple of coffee breaks every day. And with the coffee, of course, a danish in the morning and a slice of pie in the afternoon. That habit alone adds up to about 50 pounds a year.

How to break the habit of overeating

How do you break that habit? Does it take willpower? Do you feel deprived? Do you have to do without the coffee breaks?

You still enjoy your coffee breaks. You have no desire for cake to go with the coffee. In fact, if somebody puts it in front of you, it might even disgust you. You would certainly have no desire to put it in your mouth.

The power of your subconscious mind to control you is perhaps no more dramatically demonstrated than when you use H-C to turn the tables and control it.

Here is how you proceed:

1. You get into your most deeply relaxed state.

2. You get a finger levitation.

3. You deepen your state of relaxation with a countdown or other method.

4. You give your mind new instructions by visualizing yourself as you want to be. ("I see myself enjoying a coffee break with no desire for pastry or cake.")

5. You reinforce the mental image with words. ("My three meals are sufficient. They satisfy me fully. I have no need to eat between meals.")

6. You end your session.

Analyze your eating habits. Zero in on any that go over or above the three square meals a day needed. Zero in on the three meals. What happens to make them fattening? Then blast those habits to smithereens with a few H-C sessions.

You'll never miss those habits. You'll be glad to miss the weight they produce.

Slenderizing Foods Versus Fattening Foods

"Stop eating so many sweets and starches."

The voice is that of your family doctor. It could also be the voice of your grandparents' family doctor.

The fattening nature of sweets and starches has been recognized for decades. There have been all kinds of diets—the high fat diet, the high protein diet. But you'll never see a high carbohydrate diet.

The body is composed largely of protein and it needs protein to keep renewing its cells. Protein is the only one of three basic foods that it cannot manufacture from the others.

The body can make carbohydrates (energy) from fat or protein.

And it can make fat from carbohydrates or protein—you *know* it can!

But the body depends on you to feed it protein.

Protein is the number one food on your list. It is essential body maintenance material.

You also need vitamins and minerals. Many of these come in protein foods. The rest come in fresh fruits and vegetables.

Beginning to get the message?

Here are two lists of foods. List A contains fattening foods that give you more weight than nourishment. They are going to be programmed *out* of your eating way. List B contains high protein foods and foods with high mineral and vitamin content. These are the foods that keep you healthy and thin. They are going to be programmed *in.*

"OUT" LIST A (FATTENING FOODS)

Bread, rolls, crackers, and other flour products.

Noodles, macaroni, spaghetti, rice, and pastas.

Pie, cake, pastry, pancakes, waffles, ice cream, candy, rich desserts.

Jams, jellies, preserves, sugar (including substitutes containing sorbitol).

Breakfast cereals, dry or cooked.

Sauces and gravies thickened with cornstarch or flour.

Soda, beer, sweet wine, liqueurs.

"IN" LIST B (SLENDERIZING FOODS)

Beef, lamb, pork, bacon, organ meats and poultry.

Fresh-water fish, salt-water fish, shellfish, canned fish (if thoroughly drained).

Eggs, cheese (except cream cheese).

Asparagus, string and wax beans, broccoli, brussel sprouts, cabbage, celery, cucumber, kale, mushrooms, onions, peppers, tomatoes and all types of lettuce, watercress, spinach and other leafy vegetables.

Grapefruit, tangerines, melons, rhubarb, lemons.

All foods not specifically permitted on the "IN" list and not prohibited on the "OUT" list should be approached with sober caution.

How to Switch to Slenderizing Foods Without an Ounce of Willpower

Don't you wish you could feed these two lists into your mental computer and forget about them?

You can.

Here is how.

Read these lists over several times. Understand just why "OUT" foods are so labeled. Picture the "OUT" foods when you read each one. See the package of corn flakes. See the waffle, the pie, the soda in a labeled bottle. Begin to feel the sickening sweet and fattening nature of all the "OUT" foods.

When you read the "IN" list several times, see these, too. See the crisp vegetables. Taste the sizzling steak. Picture yourself on a picnic with cold chicken or slicing the Thanksgiving turkey.

Once you have thoroughly seen and felt these foods, the A list under the threat of obesity, the B list with a promise of longevity, you are ready to begin your H-C session. You will need these lists on separate pieces of paper. Copy them or photocopy them.

Here is how you program yourself into the IN foods and out of the OUT foods;

1. Place the A and B list on your lap.

2. Go into your H-C relaxation.

3. Take the A list of OUT foods and mentally dismiss them. See yourself totally disinterested in them. Say so out loud in your own words. Then crumple the list and throw it on the floor.

4. Take the B list of IN foods and mentally accept them. See yourself enjoying them, being fully satisfied with them. Say so in your own words. See yourself posting the B list on your kitchen wall.

5. End the session and post the B list in a convenient place where shopping lists and recipes are kept.

How to Attack Problem Foods That Want to Linger On

Would you believe cola for breakfast and lunch, and beer for dinner? There were some days when that was all Mr. L.L. "ate." He was an editor of textbooks for a large publishing house—a large editor at that, weighing 280 pounds at the time of his first diet aimed to prevent his hitting 300, which he felt was inevitable

He was a jovial, intelligent man, but his weight was a source of embarrassment in his work with authors. He spent overtime at the office trying to do a good job, while his wife wanted him to spend more time with the family,

H-C ran into a roadblock: the cola drinks and beer, as many as six a day, stubbornly refused to bow out of the picture. This of course, made it difficult for the chicken, fish, green vegetables, fruit and melon to enter the picture.

He was then instructed to visualize himself, while in his H-C state, drinking cola and beer and imagining that they both tasted like castor oil. He also "saw" them turning to fat as soon as they entered his body.

This did the trick. In a few sessions, he lost his taste for the two culprits and began to enjoy the "IN" foods. Last we knew, his weight was 190.

The method used is often called the obnoxious technique. Where past programming has created a persistent desire for a now unneeded food, the association of something disagreeable with that food will help unseat the deepest of seated trouble-makers.

Do you like chocolate cake? There's a beautiful, freshly baked one sitting on the table with about an inch of fudge icing. Take a closer look. It is crawling with cockroaches.

Sorry. You won't like chocolate cake as much next time, but we had to make a point.

Put such a mental image into your automatic mind, via H-C, and its effects will be stronger and more lasting.

The technique is useful where patients are having difficulty staying on special diets prescribed by their physician. Mrs. R.L. had hyperglycemia. It was absolutely essential that she avoid those foods that were going to affect her condition adversely. Yet, she kept slipping back to these foods at the risk of her health. H-C was used together with "obnoxious" associations. One by one, she licked the foods that were dangerous for her.

No Two People Become Overweight or Get Thin for the Same Reason

When it comes to slimming down, you need to give yourself personal attention.

This is difficult for many. It is so much easier to go to a doctor and say "Give me pills to lose weight."

Yet, this personal attention is vital, even with pills. Without it, you stop the pills and your weight returns. You end the diet and soon find yourself back where you started.

What do we mean by personal attention?

Well, steps one and two in this chapter involve that personal attention. You have to notice your feelings when you head for the refrigerator. Were you bored? Lonely? Worried? You have to notice how you over-eat. Double portions? Constant snacking? Beer, chocolate, soft drinks? Then you have to attack those emotions and those habits directly in H-C. Your reprogramming instructions have to be formulated to aim directly at them.

Your motivation to seek H-C help or any other means of losing weight needs to be examined, too. Discover just why you are taking action *now* to restore your proper weight and you have a powerful ally to help you get there.

W.S. was an attractive 15-year-old girl with long red hair. She was "pleasingly plump" sporting about 15 pounds of what her physician called "baby fat." She had a burning desire to be a majorette for the high school band and had studied baton twirling with a former U.S. champion since she was ten. But she was too embarrassed to try out for the position, competing against her slender girlfriends.

In H-C, she gave herself instructions that made her more confident and relaxed, that got her away from the big portions she was eating, and that programmed her for the slimming foods.

She then gave herself "majorette" instructions. She saw herself in a brief majorette uniform, slim and trim, marching energetically in front of the band. This strengthened her motivation.

Since she had always resented her mother's prodding to lose weight, she also gave herself instructions that she was staying on "IN" foods because she herself wanted to.

These two instructions were special for W.S. They probably would not apply to many other readers. But they worked wonders for her.

Give yourself personal attention. What interferes with your motivation? Then handle it in your H-C reprogramming. What strengthens your motivation? Then add this to your H-C reprogramming.

Six Short Steps to the World of the Slender

Put the book down now, relax, and see yourself thin.

You have just taken the first step to become the attractive slender person you want to be.

Step two, three, and four have been spelled out in this chapter.

Step two—tailor your attitudes.

Step three—reprogram the quantity and frequency of food in your eating habits.

Step four—program yourself out of OUT foods and in to IN foods.

Step five is to strengthen your motivation as described in the previous section.

Step six is to keep a progress chart.

This progress chart is a useful way of reinforcing your sense of accomplishment, your forward movement toward a weight goal.

Place it on the wall of your bathroom. At the top left, let it show your present weight. Vertical lines are each week. Horizontal lines are each five pounds. Put a big dot at the lower right, showing the weight you want to reach and the week you want this to happen.

Watch the line descend.

It is your lifeline. The lower it goes, the longer you live.

And the happier.

How to Get Results for Yourself from Chapter 17 Now

Feel like something to eat? Why? Is it hunger, or some other type of emotional appetite? Dig for it. Identify it. H-C it out. Then proceed with tailoring your attitudes and reprogramming your foods toward the high nourishment, low fattening spectrum. Weight disappears effortlessly and for good.

18 – HOW TO QUIT SMOKING PERMANENTLY THE EASY WAY-KEY TO ALL HABIT BREAKING

What to Expect in This Chapter

Anybody can stop smoking. And stop and stop. Here's how to stop once and for all—no sweat, no "withdrawal symptoms." What's more, the same principles apply to other habits you are ready to kiss goodbye.

Smoking is going strong despite the U.S. Surgeon General's repeated warnings. Cigarette sales did not lose a step when health warnings went on the packages or when television ads were banned.

It looks as if smoking is here to stay ... along with emphysema, lung cancer, indirect damage to the heart, circulation system and other vital organs, not to speak of yellow teeth and nails, breath and body odor, nuisance to others, and fire damage in and out of the house.

Now, however, another by-product of cigarette smoking promises to give smokers second thoughts, especially women smokers, if the discovery of a California physician gets properly publicized: smoking cigarettes can age the skin, especially on the face, by some 20 years.

Dr. Harry W. Daniell studied over one thousand patients and friends, scoring them on facial wrinkles. In every ten year age group, heavy smokers were much more likely to be heavily wrinkled than non-smokers. Even long after the heavy smokers had given up the habit, their telltale wrinkles lingered on. The most heavily wrinkled group were all smokers.

Add personal vanity to the list of valid motivating reasons for you to drop the smoking habit today.

Cigarettes Smoke You

You are programmed to smoke.

It probably didn't take you long to do it—possibly a few days or a few weeks. But now you don't even think about it when you do it.

You reach for the pack, pop a cigarette in your mouth, grab the matches or lighter, light up, take a deep drag, flick occasionally, puff occasionally, crush it out. You never consciously think of the fact that you are smoking. It is all automatic—pretty much like typing a letter, or driving home in the car, while you're busy thinking of something else.

In effect, the cigarette is smoking you.

The only time you ever think about smoking is when the subconscious mind is threatened by a low supply. The automatic mind depends on your logical, conscious mind to provide that supply. It keeps reminding you, "Do you have enough? Shouldn't you pick up a couple of packs as long as you are at this counter?" Or, "Better stop on your way to the office."

Sometimes it even pushes the panic button: "My God, that was my last cigarette!"

But while you're smoking, there's little conscious awareness after that first puff. One physician is telling his smoking patients to carry a little pill box and a cuticle scissors around with them. Whenever they take that first puff, clip off the glowing end, and save the rest of the cigarette. Then the next time they light up, do the same thing. Result, 90% of the satisfaction and only 10% of the trouble.

The idea is good. But we feel you ought to take the bull by the proverbial horns and demand your full emancipation.

You can have it, you know. When you try that prison door, you'll see it was never locked.

Make Smoking a Conscious Activity

The way to start is to make smoking a conscious activity. Reclaim it from your automatic mind. Say in effect, "I'm taking this function over for a period just to re-evaluate it."

Then, alert yourself to this conscious awareness the moment you reach. Watch yourself go through every motion. Watch yourself experience that first drag. Be aware of how you feel exhaling it.

How long before the next puff? How are you holding the cigarette? How does the second puff compare with the first? How does the smoke taste? How does it feel in your throat? In your lungs? What does it look like after you exhale? Is the ash long enough to flick yet? Follow yourself all the way down to the butt.

S.I. Hayakawa, president of San Francisco State College, broke a 30-year addiction by just becoming conscious of his smoking. He started to take notes. How many cigarettes had he enjoyed? Which puffs were the best? Then he began to consider himself a non-smoker. It took three months. But that's what he became.

Just the way obtaining a physical finger levitation in your Hypno-Cybernetic sessions creates communication between your conscious and your automatic mind, so will the consciousness of smoking establish these communications. If you do this first, your H-C commands will be doubly effective.

There is another advantage. Once you are conscious of smoking, you can be conscious of its assets as well as its liabilities. You can surely derive more satisfaction being aware of the act of smoking than if you lit up, smoked, and doused it like an automaton, which is the way most people smoke.

Besides being aware of what the smoke is doing *for* you, you can also be aware of what the smoke is doing *to* you.

Look at the cigarette. Do your really need the taste of it? Picture the black, leathery texture of your lungs that the smoke has been causing. Compare it to the healthy pink lungs of the non-smoker. ("How can my blood renew its oxygen supply properly?") Be aware of each puff. What is it doing to you? How much residue was left behind in your lungs by that smoke you just exhaled? Then when you douse it—was it worth it?

Be conscious, too, of how many cigarettes you smoke each day, when you smoke them, where you buy them, how much they cost.

By this conscious critical analysis, you are helping to reprogram yourself. Your automatic mind smokes, you don't. It has been told smoking is great. Now you are telling it otherwise.

This won't help you enjoy the smoke. But it's better than shock treatment.

Schick Laboratories in Seattle runs a stop smoking clinic built around mild shock treatment therapy. The smoker is hooked up to a small box designed to administer a mild electric shock. He is told to light up, and as he does so, a jolt of current hits his wrists through the electrodes strapped to them. It is somewhat like getting a shock of static electricity after scuffling across a carpet.

The smoker is asked to smoke two cigarettes in the hour-long session, 15 puffs on each. That means he is "zapped" thirty times. This helps to produce an aversion to cigarettes. One reporter who tried the system went from a pack-per-day to a non-smoker in five sessions. Two months later, she found it hard even to walk near the therapy room.

This aversion therapy is the same as the obnoxious technique used in chapter 17 to break the hold on you of certain foods.

It works. But there is an easier way.

A Smoker Today—a Non-Smoker Tomorrow

"OK. Everybody light up."

"An all-day, stop smoking clinic is taking place in a large hotel. The hypnologist has spent the morning teaching Hypno-Cybernetic methods of inducing a deep state of relaxation and contacting the automatic mind via finger and hand levitation."

Everybody has been encouraged to smoke during the morning session; that is, in a "conscious" way, being aware of the pleasure, if any, and the problems. The meeting room is littered with ash trays overflowing with butts.

Now the afternoon session is beginning. This is the "business" end of the clinic. Participants are putting themselves into an H-C state. The hypnologist is now reciting a list of instructions which they are repeating to themselves as H-C reprogramming.

He pauses after each:

> I remember the dark brown taste in my mouth.
>
> I remember the harshness of the cigarette.
>
> I see the yellow on my teeth and fingertips.
>
> I see the nicotine stains on my clothing.
>
> I remember the near fires my smoking has caused.
>
> I know the coughing and phlegm caused by smoking.
>
> I know the fear of lung cancer and will have this fear as long as I smoke.

I know the damage to my lungs, heart, and circulatory system caused by smoking.

I know my mouth smells of tobacco and is distasteful to others.

I know my smoking is a social affrontery to many.

Now the hypnologist is switching to positive instructions. As he does so, an assistant is moving quietly around the room removing ash trays and butts. The door is opened so that the smoke-filled room can air out.

I now see myself as a non-smoker.

My lungs require only fresh, clean air.

My health improves, free of the deterrent of tobacco.

I enjoy the taste of food so much more.

I am free of the fear of emphysema or lung cancer.

I am free of the need to keep supplied with cigarettes and lights.

My house is a safer and healthier place to live.

I breathe better, smell better, feel better.

I am socially and sexually a more attractive person.

I *am* a non-smoker.

The hypnologist ends the session:

OK. Everybody light up.

Not a hand reaches for a cigarette. Cigarettes have vanished from the scene, literally and figuratively. The air of the room is clean. No smell of stale smoke, dead butts.

A couple of hours later, there have been several reinforcement sessions. Everybody feels like a non-smoker You can see the relief on their faces.

I am a non-smoker.

No ands, ifs, or buts.

How to Stay a Non-Smoker

You can give yourself these ten negative pictures and ten positive pictures by doing several H-C sessions and using a few at
a time. Or you may memorize them and go right through the
whole sequence of pictures at one H-C session. No matter if you
forget one or two. Check over the above list each time you do a
session.

How about doing such an H-C session right now?

To stay a non-smoker, two H-C steps must be taken:

1. You must repeat the above H-C session daily for one
   week, then taper off to once a week for several weeks.

2. You must give yourself tension relaxing instructions.

Programming for a tension-free life is what this book is all
about.

Most chapters contain suitable phraseology to use, especially
chapters 4, 14, and 16.

You can provide a step-by-step method to assure progress toward an ultimate self-mastery goal.

Start with instructions for *relaxation.*

Then use instructions for *calmness.*

Follow with instructions for *composure.*

Later use instructions for *confidence.*

Graduate to instructions for *self-assurance.*

And wind up with affirmations of *self-control.*

The frequency of these tension-relaxing instructions for your
automatic mind is determined by how you feel.

Mrs. K.G. had been a very heavy smoker. Because of her physician's warnings, she had stopped for a number of years through the use of a hypnosis method similar to H-C. Then came a serious emotional experience that caused her to reach for a cigarette. Instantly, she realized the danger of becoming addicted again. She reached for the telephone to call the hypnologist she had originally worked with. He was away on a two-week vacation.

So, instead, as she says, "I had a ball." She went back to cigarettes as never before. Soon she was in the hospital with asthma and emphysema. The doctors gave her only a slim chance to pull through. She did, though, and took up H-C which put the reins in her own hands to prevent another relapse.

Once you are a non-smoker, you can stay that way by using H-C reinforcement programming at the first thought of a cigarette.

Go through all of the mental instructions given in this chapter once again, just as if you were a smoker.

Chances are you will not think of a cigarette for another long while.

Every day that you are a non-smoker deepens the programming as a non-smoker.

You gradually become an habitual non-smoker.

Other Techniques to Quit Smoking with H-C

There are aversion or obnoxious techniques you can use for smoking that don't require a little electrical shock every time you light up.

You can give yourself the instructions in H-C that a cigarette tastes like excrement.

Or you can give yourself the instructions in H-C that cigarette smoke smells like burnt rubber.

Or you can actually sniff from a bottle of ammonia as you instruct your automatic mind to take note.

And would you believe that weevils love tobacco and can you imagine how they taste, shredded and burnt?

There is also a tapering-off technique that is often used successfully. The smoker figures out his average time between cigarettes by dividing his waking hours into the total number of cigarettes consumed in an average smoking day. For instance, two packs in a 16-hour day means two and one half cigarettes every hour, or a cigarette every 24 minutes.

In H-C reprogramming, the instruction is given that this 24-minute interval will now be one hour. After a few days at this longer interval between smokes, the interval is increased to two hours. When the daily consumption is down to one or two cigarettes, it can be continued or further reduced to one a week, and so on.

In using these methods, you must continue to give relaxation instructions to induce composure and confidence. These help to reduce "withdrawal" symptoms.

Sometimes what is known as a symptom substitute is also helpful to bridge the gap. Chewing gum and hard candies are popular for this purpose, as are dummy cigarettes made of chocolate.

Whatever method is used, you the smoker must see yourself as a non-smoker "as if" it were true, with expectation and belief.

How to Use H-C to End Other Unwanted Habits

Habits are programming.

Willpower is energy.

When you pit even the strongest willpower against habits, it's like matching the irresistible force with the unmovable body.

Habits are programming.

H-C is programming.

When you pit H-C against habits, they don't have a chance. Their programming is being reprogrammed.

Like the man who said, "You can't fire me." So they didn't. They just did away with his job.

You can do away with any habit you no longer want by just reprogramming away the job it does.

As an example, take liquor. It fills a need, does a job.

If you reprogram yourself through H-C to have the need no longer, you do away with liquor's job.

Give yourself positive suggestions that enable you to cope with the problems that are at the root of excessive drinking. That means you need to identify the problems—work, home, other—then attack them head-on with instructions to the effect:

> I am resourceful. I can handle _____. I am capable of
> _____. I am strong, efficient, sociable without liquor.

Couple this with the obnoxious technique and you give liquor a one, two punch:

> Liquor now tastes like castor oil.

Be sure to use as your obnoxious material something that you know the taste of and do detest.

Another obnoxious technique can be tied right in with the liquor:

> From this moment on, any small quantity of liquor will make me feel just as sick as I have felt from large quantities.

A reinforcing technique is to review the benefits of not drinking. Do this the same way as the smoker does. See the road ahead if you continue to be a heavy drinker—the deteriorating health, the memory black-outs, loss of job effectiveness. Then see the road ahead as a non-drinker—longer life, social acceptance, job efficiency.

Another reinforcing technique for any habit is the relaxation, calmness, composure, confidence, self-assurance, and self-control progressive H-C instructions previously described.

The positive suggestion is always the best.

As for nail-biting. It helps to compare ugly hands with beautiful hands, but just the one instruction, "I can have beautiful hands," "I see myself with beautiful hands," "My beautiful hands are important to me," can turn the trick.

Symptom substitution should be kept in mind, too. "Every time I want a drink, I reach for a _____ (glass of soda, water, milk, or peppermint, etc.).

The One Trick That a Dying Habit Can Play to Survive

Habits die hard.

They need the multi-faceted approach because they have developed in that manner themselves:

- Positive personality reinforcement.
- See yourself without the habit.
- Make the habit obnoxious.
- Induce calmness, confidence, self-control.
- See the benefits.
- Substitute acceptable symptoms.

Despite these six reprogrammings, you may reach for a drink, a cigarette, or a nail to bite.

You say immediately with conviction and belief, "It didn't work!"

What you have just done is cancelled the H-C programming. The stronger your feeling and the greater your conviction, the cleaner the job of cancelling you did.

Sometimes, when a hypnologist gives a hypnotized subject a test for the effectiveness of suggestions, he says, "You cannot lift your right arm." The subject is then instructed to try to lift his arm. He might lift it with effort. His first thought then is, "I failed. Hypnotism is not working for me."

Hypnotism and H-C work for everybody. Hypnotism works better for some than for others, depending on the depth of relaxation. The hypnotist knows this but the subject doesn't. What he is doing inadvertently when he says "It doesn't work" is giving himself suggestions opposite to those of the hypnologist.

So the hypnologist looks ahead and leaves the door slightly open. Instead of saying "You cannot lift your right arm," he says, "You will have great difficulty raising your right arm."

You can also leave the door open. See if you can figure out a way to do this without issuing an invitation to the habit to stick around.

> From time to time I may feel the urge to _____. This is just the echo. It means little to me. I can cope with it.

Effects of H-C on the Drug Habit

All habits are more successfully dealt with early in the game. You may be an excellent Hypno-Cyberneticist. But you have had much more practice making habits.

Also, although habits can be deeply etched, your H-C instructions might be only lightly etched if your relaxation is not as blissfully deep as it could be.

Even the hard drug habit will respond to H-C if caught early enough.

The procedure is the same as described for other habits. Use a multi-pronged attack on the emotional and symptomatic levels. Increase self-confidence. Create repulsion.

One aspect of breaking the hard drug habit is the withdrawal symptoms. Every drug addict knows these symptoms because they begin when a "fix" wears off. The fear of them compounds the terror.

This is perhaps where H-C is most effective on the drug scene.

You can use H-C to render withdrawal symptoms less of a problem. There are two ways.

1. You can give yourself the H-C instruction that you will have amnesia during the time of the withdrawal symptoms.

2. You can induce withdrawal symptoms in advance of the crisis, handle them, and condition yourself to cope with the main event.

In the first instance, you go through the agonies of withdrawal and are not mentally aware of them. It is similar to the analgesia created in chapter 15, except not at the nerve level but at the memory bank, or mind, level.

In the second instance, you invite the symptoms in advance and then end them. In this way you build up confidence that you can handle them. The fear and tension are removed and this alone can alleviate the ordeal considerably.

Let's hope few readers need to use H-C for this purpose, but it is there if required. Much more research needs to be done. Undoubtedly, H-C bears tremendous promise for drug addicts in the future.

How to Get Results for Yourself from Chapter 18 Now

You can break any habit you have made. In making them you have programmed yourself to use the habit to fill an emotional need, to like the feel or taste of the habit, and to depend on the habit. Now you reverse the process. You identify the emotional need and program yourself to be sufficient in that department, you program yourself to dislike the feel or taste, and you program yourself to be independent of the habit and reliant on your own resources. Smoking, excess drinking, and other unwanted habits are making you behave in a way that can ruin your health and happiness. Use H-C to reprogram yourself out of them today. Relax. Get a finger levitation. Do it now.

19 – HOW TO RID YOURSELF OF INSOMNIA

What to Expect from This Chapter

Sleepless nights can become a habit. There is no need to lie awake when you could be enjoying blessed sleep night after night. H-C programs you into a deep sleep the very first try. In fact, some who try fall asleep before they have completed their first session.

Did you know that you can be programmed *not* to fall asleep?

Here's how it goes.

You go to bed and become aware that you are still awake. You watch for the moment when you will fall asleep. Of course, while you watch it doesn't happen. So you get anxious. You tense up. You try to fall asleep. Finally, you give up the whole process in the wee hours of the morning. And you sleep.

But the memory banks have been alerted. Next time you hit the bed you wonder whether you will fall asleep. Becoming self-conscious about sleep keeps you awake. The whole cycle is repeated. Now you're in line for a habit.

Three times is the charm. You become an insomniac. It's a big club. Some three million toss and turn with you every night.

Can the process be reversed by programming?

Of course it can.

Three H-C Exercises that Prepare
You for a Good Night's Rest

You have already learned three procedures that have proved to be all some insomniacs need to end their nightly ordeals: One—deep relaxation. Two—quieting the mind. Three—deepening the relaxed stage.

If you have turned to this chapter first because sleep is your top priority problem, it will be necessary for you to read chapter 3 and learn how to induce contact with your subconscious mind.

It will also be necessary to read chapter 14 and learn techniques for pacifying the mind.

We will use a special means of deepening relaxation but it won't hurt to read chapter 10 where techniques for this are given.

Mrs. L.W. never had to use any reprogramming to end her insomnia. She got into bed; went into an H-C state of deep relaxation; visualized her favorite passive scene—a grassy meadow; then started to count herself deeper. She changed the procedure here, though. Instead of starting at 500 and going backwards, which will be recommended in the pages ahead, she started at one and counted sheep jumping over a pole fence. She seldom got to more than twenty.

Others may have to use specific instructions to the automatic mind to change anti-sleep patterns. But everyone should try the relaxation first.

Again, the steps are:

1. Go into a deep H-C state when in bed.

2. Pacify the mind.

3. Deepen the stage by a countdown.

The countdown from 500 backwards is quite effective. Few

people have to get to 400, but if you do, don't be concerned because any... moment... now... you'll... be... feeling... drowsier... and...

Record This and Play It on Retiring

If you have a recorder, you can program your subconscious mind to accept sleep by talking to yourself when you turn in.

Read the following monologue into the recorder authoritatively as if you were talking to a child. But speak without emotion, in a monotone, and as slowly as you can without it sounding unnatural.

> You are now comfortable and ready for deep. Get into a favorite sleeping position and listen to my voice. You become heavier. You pay less and less attention to everything else around you. You listen to me count. One... you are becoming more and more drowsy now. Each number makes you drowsier... sleepier... two ... drowsy ... heavy ... heavy... deeper and deeper... three ... you are becoming more and more sleepy now ... more and more sleepy ... more and more drowsy ... four... you are going deeper and deeper to sleep ... nothing will disturb you ... you will only want to listen to my voice ... each moment you are going deeper asleep... with each word you are going deeper and deeper asleep ... five ... deep ... deep ... asleep. I want you to visualize a long staircase ... a safe, comfortable staircase ... soon I will count backwards ... each number will take you further and further down the staircase and as you go back down and down you will go still deeper and deeper asleep. And as you do, you will begin to notice that you have less sensation of feeling. You will begin to notice that nothing disturbs you ... that you have no desire to do anything at all. I'm going to count back ... ten ... imagine the staircase ... you are beginning to go down and down ... as you do, you have less and less sensation ... less and less feeling. There's a feeling of gradual numbness all around you ... you feel less and less... you take notice of less and less... nothing bothers you ... you only want to hear my voice ... my voice makes you drowsier... sleepier... you are more and more relaxed ... more and more relaxed ... drifting down deeper and deeper... nine ... you continue to go deeper asleep... deeper asleep as I talk to you ... going down and down... as if you

were floating, floating, drifting ... eight... seven ...lower and lower ... you now have no desire to move ... six ... you have no desire to speak ... no desire to speak... five... you have no desire to move or to speak or to do anything ... you now only want to sleep... deeper and deeper... four ... the feeling of relaxation is pleasant to you ... you are enjoying it very much... you want nothing to disturb your state ... three ... getting deeper and deeper ... down and down and down... two ... drifting lower and lower... deeper and deeper... one ... just sleep now ... there is nothing else for you to do ... nothing else is required of you... I shall stop talking now for a few moments. During these few moments you will go deeper and deeper asleep... when I speak to you again it will not startle you... it will not awaken you, but it will enable you to go even deeper and deeper asleep. Just sleep now until I talk to you again... just sleep now... (pause 30 seconds).

You are deep asleep now but you can go even deeper asleep ... even deeper than you are now because it is a very pleasant experience ... because it will be very beneficial to you ... you are going to sleep much more deeply ... once again I will count and you will go into an even deeper sleep ... you will begin to sink into a much much deeper sleep and at the count of five you will be very, very sound asleep .., one ... you are going to go deeply ... much more deeply asleep ... two ... you are going deeper and deeper asleep ... with each count you sink deeper asleep ... with each word I say, you sink deeper asleep ... with each breath that you take, you go more deeply asleep ... three ... sleep ... deeply ... soundly ... sleep... my voice makes you want to sleep... always deeper and deeper... you can feel yourself sinking into very, very deep sleep... sinking... sinking into a deeper and sounder sleep in which you pay attention to nothing but my voice which begins to sound as if it were coming from far away ... four ... you continue to go deeper asleep as I count... as I talk to you ... even as I talk to you now you are going deeper and deeper asleep ... continue to sleep... at the next count you will be deeply... soundly asleep ... five ... deep ... deep asleep ... deep ... deep. You are so comfortable ... you allow this comfortable situation to drift into a deeper and deeper sleep, into a more and more profound sleep ... there is a feeling of dullness all over you ... your legs, your arms, your whole body feels dull... you have no interest in moving or speaking or doing anything... you have less and less sensation ... less and less feeling ... less and less interest... you only want to sleep... to sleep more and more deeply, more and more soundly ... sleep deeper and deeper.... Nothing will disturb you, you will remain asleep until your normal time for awakening... nothing will disturb you ... nothing at all... just sleep now ... just sleep.

Six Common Reasons for Insomnia or Fitful Sleep and How to Deprogram Them Out of Your Life

Mrs. S.G. was a worrier. She worried about keeping her appointments with the authors and, because she spent so much time worrying, often missed them. But she did come in three times, enough to learn H-C and the countdown method, and then to deprogram herself out of her worrisome nature.

She gave herself instructions that "everything happens for the best," that she is "capable of handling any eventualities," and that she is always "cool, calm, and confident." She reported. She used a 300 count back and the first time could remember only 275.

Worry is a sleep wrecker.

So is anxiety.

So is pressure.

So is tenseness.

So is depression.

And so is fear.

Now you see why some of the ego strengthening suggestions given in the previous chapters are useful in the H-C handling of insomnia.

Here are some that overlap with what has gone before but which have been worded to bear more precisely on the sleeping problem:

- Every day I become stronger and more self-reliant.
- My nerves are strong and steady.

- My mind is less and less pre-occupied with myself.
- I am calm, composed, tranquil.
- I am less and less easily upset or apprehensive.
- I see things in true perspective night and day.
- I am happy,, optimistic, and not easily depressed.
- I am independent, confident and in control.
- My mind and body are in repose. I am perfectly at ease.
- When I say 'relax now,' I attain a state on the brink of sleep.

Select the mental instructions you feel are appropriate for you. Get into your H-C state during daylight hours, deepen your state, then program yourself with one or more of these strengthening and tranquilizing affirmations.

Some Special Lie-Awake Situations

Miss M.L. was on heavy medication for her insomnia. She was "out" most of the night, but the pills were making her days one long "daze." She was dopey until mid-afternoon and found it hard to function. Yet, if she did not take the pills she would be too tired the next day to function.

In H-C, she used the countdown method to sleep as well as instructions that she could reduce the number of pills.

She was soon able to get off the pills in a permissive way. That is, if she ever felt she needed one she could take it. At last word, she was neither a pill addict nor an insomniac.

In another situation, a middle-aged woman, married to a physician, had a multitude of physical complaints. He would get angry, accusing her of bidding for his attention and being a hypochondriac. She had pains in her hands, pains in her feet, in her abdomen, and legs. She had double vision, stomach spasms, continuous headaches, and ... insomnia.

When she came for H-C help, it was for the insomnia. There

was no desire to seek relief from the other "ailments," yet the insomnia was due largely to their effect on her. Not wanting to deprive her of her only emotional defense against what was to her a painful marital situation, the H-C approach she was given was that she might not "recover" from all these complaints, but she would be able to cope with them better, to survive, and to continue to live with them all. She also gave herself the following reinforcing instructions:

> I will be far less preoccupied with my feelings.
>
> I will be more and more independent, able to stand up on my own two feet.
>
> Every day I will be physically stronger and fitter, emotionally stronger and fitter.

The first thing to improve was her sleep. One by one, then, all her "ailments" disappeared.

H-C is easy to apply for the average person who learns to use it. However, insomnia is often one ailment that demands ingenuity in H-C application. Everybody lies awake for a different reason. It may all add up to a self-consciousness about sleep, but the programming that causes this, and which cries to be deprogrammed, can be as different in two people as day and night.

One woman could not relax enough to get very far with a Hypno-Cybernetic approach. She seemed to have a defiant attitude. When she announced each time, "It's not working," there was a triumphant note in her voice.

It was decided to reverse procedures in her case. She was instructed to fidget as much as possible in H-C and feel as nervous and as tense as she could while she gave herself the mental instruction, "I will try to stay awake tonight as long as I can," The H-C session went better than before. That night she managed to force her eyes to stay open for about five minutes before conking off to a good night's sleep.

Her defiance had been harnessed to go to work for her instead of against her.

Changes in H-C procedures are not often that "about faced" but they do often require an individualized approach.

How to Feel Twice as Good on Half the Sleep

If you were to bet a natural sleeper, who is usually off the minute his head touches the pillow, a million dollars that he can't fall asleep in five minutes, you'll win. Whenever a person becomes self-conscious about sleep, he is putting up a splendid barricade.

The problem of lost sleep then compounds itself. The less sound the sleep, the more nervous and troubled are the thoughts. Added to daytime worries are the worries about what this lack of sleep will do to health and energy.

The solution is often found in changing sleep habits. Try going to bed at different times, even if it's just for a cat nap.

Before taking a nap, go into an H-C session and give your automatic mind the following instruction:

> I will fail asleep readily when I now begin my count-back method.
>
> My nap will be thoroughly refreshing and my energy will be recharged.

In your sleep position start counting backward slowly from 500.

Another way to combat the effects of loss of sleep, so as to better attack the insomnia itself, is to program your mind to utilize sleep at a more efficient rate.

Edison got along fine on four hours of sleep. You don't have to be an electronic genius to need this little sleep. Many people have unwillingly programmed themselves to thrive on just a few hours of sleep per night. The mind will compensate for late hours of TV viewing, reading, or other recreation. It will accomplish in four hours what it would do in eight hours.

You can instruct your mind to do exactly this and thus remove one of the by-products of insomnia. The specific programming is this:

> I see myself getting a full night's rest in four hours. At the end of four hours of sleep, my body is fully renewed, my mind rested, and my energy replenished. I am thoroughly revitalized in body and mind with four hours of sleep.

We don't want to leave you with the belief that insomnia is difficult to treat with H-C. It is really one of the easiest problems to solve. As mentioned before, it often responds to the relaxed H-C state without any reprogramming necessary.

However, where it is stubborn, it is valuable to know the many faces of insomnia.

Sleep is the reward for activity. It is yours to claim. As Leigh Hunt said, "It is a delicious moment, certainly, that of being well-nestled in bed and feeling that you shall drop gently to sleep. The good is to come, not past...."

How to Get Results for Yourself from Chapter 19 Now

Tense your hands, letting the fingers clench in a tight fist. Now relax them. Do this with your jaw, your legs, your eyelids. Each time get to know what "relaxed" feels like. Now go into an H-C session in bed on retiring. Relax. Get a finger levitation. Deepen your relaxation. Now start counting backward slowly from 500. Pleasant dreams. Later use H-C to program out worry and tension and program in self-confidence and composure to make your sleep come on even more quickly and to be even more restful.

20 – HOW TO TURN THE TIDE OF ADVERSITY IN YOUR FAVOR

What to Expect in This Chapter

This is what Hypno-Cybernetics is all about. Nobody likes to swim constantly against the tide. Here is how to get what you want from life with the tide of good fortune sweeping with you.

The state of blissful repose that we attain in a Hypno-Cybernetic session is the same that a person assumes in deep thought, prayer, meditation, yoga, reflection, contemplation, and silence.

It is what scientists now recognize as the alpha brain wave state. It is a state where the human mind, one ninth conscious, the other eight-ninths subconscious, responds as though these two realms were no longer divided. The conscious mind *reaches* the subconscious mind.

This is the same state of mind used in Dr. Grantley Dick-Read's method of natural childbirth and in many systems of programmed motivation, where the listener is led through audio recordings to new principles of personal effectiveness and success. It is the state of mind that brings you all the benefits of hypnosis, auto-conditioning, and mental control.

The better you are able to reach this blissful state of deep repose, the greater a miracle maker you become in shaping your life.

How to Go In and Out of Your H-C State Walking Down the Street in Ten Seconds

It has been essential for you to go through the sitting or lying positions, the mental and physical relation, and the finger levitation procedure in order to remove the conscious mind as a watchman and protector of the subconscious.

However, now that you have mastered this method, you can program yourself for instant return to this mental state, no matter where you are or what you are doing. You can give yourself the needed "shot in the arm" ("I am capable. I am successful."), and then end your session and nobody will have noticed you.

Here is what you must do.

Each time you practice H-C at home, give yourself the following programming:

> Every time I say or think the word Hypno-Cybernetics, I instantly attain this same quiet state of mind. I give myself instructions and I end my state by saying or thinking one, two, three.

Why not do this right now along with other programming you are working on?

You don't have to use the word Hypno-Cybernetics. You can, instead, use a private code word known only to you. A word like Hypno-Cybernetics which is getting to be better known every day can come up in conversations. Yes, that's right. You get a momentary far-away look in your eyes... until you count one, two, three. So you may feel better about a concocted word known only to yourself.

The beauty of the one word method of Hypno-Cybernetic induction is that you can obtain on-the-spot results to combat any situation that arises. It may be a return of some urge to take up a habit you have broken. It may be a feeling of pessimism or just being "down in the dumps." It may be the need for that extra push or stick-to-it-iveness.

Whatever the need, you say "Hypno-Cybernetics." You give yourself appropriate instructions—to reinforce the habit control, to send your feelings high with hope and expectation, or to provide you with that extra measure of self-confidence and self-mastery. You count one, two, three.

You can even shorten the procedure by doing what the authors have done: shorten Hypno-Cybernetics to H-C.

Things You Can Do with H-C That Seem Impossible

"Just a few minutes with this amazing course shows you how to put yourself at ease in seconds—even in the most nerve-racking situations!"

So reads an advertisement in a national magazine for one of the many audio systems now being sold. It is based on attaining the alpha level of the mind which you have already learned to do in this book.

The H-C method, as you have seen, is incredibly simple to learn and this book has devoted only one chapter to it. The rest of the nineteen chapters have been focused on the many areas of everyday living in which you can use H-C and how.

Life has more than nineteen areas to it. Even nine hundred and nineteen chapters couldn't possibly do a complete job. The tide of adversity has a myriad of wavelets and it takes a myriad of counter-wavelets to turn that tide.

Here are some uses of H-C that have either not been covered or not specifically mentioned. The list is meant for you to read and for you then to add any of your own personal uses that the list may bring to mind.

There can be no end to this list, though in this book, end it must:

- Turn on H-C in the middle of a conversation in order to

remember everything that is being said without having to take notes.

- Use your H-C state to solve a difficult math problem that would otherwise take an inordinate amount of time.

- Turn on your personal magnetism with a flick of your H-C at a critical moment, when you want somebody to do something for you.

- Scan the dictionary in your H-C state and each time add scores of words to your power to communicate.

- Stop your show of bad temper or irritation in its tracks.

- Double your reading speed by programming your mind to accept the meanings faster.

- Program yourself to visualize the solution to any problem, every hour on the hour, so that you stop momentarily, automatically, to give energy to that solution, bringing it about faster.

- Use H-C to stop a stubborn case of hiccups. Serenity of body, mind, and breathing does it.

- Use H-C to ease the discomfort of having to go to the bathroom, until the facilities are available.

- Use H-C to end snoring, nose-picking, bedwetting, kleptomania, and any other antisocial habit.

- Be a psycho-surgeon. Cut out any persistent thought that "bugs" you.

- Elevate your sales enthusiasm moments before you make a sales contact.

- Program yourself for statesmanship at a meeting, just before you walk in.

- Use a shot of H-C to make yourself come to life at a party.

- Give yourself a moment of H-C programming when your feet hit the floor in the morning, to make the day go right.

- Use H-C to help you win the game, be it football or bridge.

- Use H-C to remove a sudden embarrassing facial tic or other physical spasm.

- Strengthen your courage instantly, at a moment of fear or panic.

- While waiting for a decision, use H-C to strengthen your knowledge that whatever the decision is, you can handle it and make it happen for the best.

- Exhausted? Say, "H-C." Then visualize yourself getting the restful effects of three hours of sleep within three seconds. Then say one, two, three.

Add a few more personal uses to this list right now.

Do an H-C session and program yourself to remember to use H-C for these special personal uses. Right now.

How to Let H-C in to Help the Secret "You" Whom Nobody Else Knows

In the United States today, there are some eleven million households which consist of only one person, an increase of over 50 percent in ten years. Most of these "loners," according to census statistics, are women residing alone in big cities.

However, millions of other people live "alone." They may be surrounded by family but they are so deep within themselves, other people do not penetrate.

A waitress once remarked that she can see things about people merely by the way they choose a table. Some pick a table where they can be seen, others where they are less conspicuous. Some like to sit near the door they entered so they can exit quickly in case of fire or other emergency. Some like to be against a wall; it gives them a more comfortable, not-stared-at feeling. One man likes to sit where he can keep his eyes on a clock. A woman likes to have a table close to the ladies' restroom. Near the music, near a window, away from the bustling kitchen, in view of the entrance so they can see who comes in—all are personal preferences, reflecting individual idiosyncrasies, signposts pointing to the nature of the inner person.

The inner person has a private universe. These are the secret feelings and fantasies that nobody dare intrude on.

- You will know what is just and you will be just and fair in the treatment of others. You respect their rights as well as your own.

- You see the universal purpose and perceive progress toward that purpose, despite all semblances of adversity.

The secret *you* wants these things. Use H-C to open the inner door and let it all in.

How to Be an Effective Near-Sighted Visionary

Not all visionaries are far-sighted enough to change the world.

In fact, most visionaries are quite near-sighted.

They cannot see beyond their own business, warehouse or factory. But that's far enough to devise a new system for production control or a new system for office routing or for work scheduling.

Thomas Edison said, "Genius is one percent inspiration and 99 percent perspiration." Notice, he put inspiration first, even though he was singing a song of elbow grease, physical effort, and perseverance.

When the manager of a canning plant that was short of space heard that a plastic boat manufacturer was vacating its quarters, his colleagues told him not to waste his time examining the place. Impractical to convert, they said. But he went anyway. He found it had a rail spur. The truck loading facilities were just right. Where plastic was processed he saw metal being processed. Where boats and equipment were being assembled, he visualized his plant's canning procedure fitting in perfectly. And where the boats were being stored for shipment, he saw that with very little additional construction his plant's finished products could be stored.

He then needed to carry his visual image a step forward. He got a set of blueprints of the plastic boat plant and sketched on a tissue overlay how he saw his own plant's space requirements fitting in. His colleagues were convinced, and in four months they were moved in and operating efficiently.

He may never have heard of H-C, yet, whenever he was relaxed and visualizing, he was using it.

You may be even more "near-sighted" than this plant manager. You may be able to visualize only an improved office layout. Or maybe only a better filing system.

Some people may be able to visualize just how to add another bedroom on to their present home. Others may not be able to see any further than a more neatly arranged closet.

The important thing is not how much you can see in your mental imaging, but how well you can see it. A sharp mental image of what you would like to happen is the "shadow of a coming event" and the very "substance of things to come." With H-C you sharpen your image and you program it deeper into your mind.

Focus that image. See the detail. See it live. And it will.

You Can Have Anything You Want If

You Can See Yourself Having It

Do you want something?

You can have it.

If there are feelings and fantasies that interfere with your comfort and effectiveness, you can use H-C privately to program them out of your life.

If there are feelings and fantasies that contribute to your comfort and effectiveness, you can program new strength into them, and make them more meaningful and real.

In West Germany, there is now a tour to the orient for men only. Beate Uhse, notorious sex queen, has arranged these tours to satisfy the male's dream vacation with a beautiful, exotic hostess catering to his every wish in Hong Kong, Tokyo, and Bangkok. Needless to say, these geisha, massage, and dancing girl tours are immensely popular and catching on in other parts of the world.

Whatever your secret dream – yes, even if it is of dancing girls – you can make it come true.

How? Get into your H-C session. See it coming true.

Don't just dream it or fantasize it all over again. But visualize your bags packed if it is a trip, or her in your arms in the precise spot you want it to happen, or him popping the question with a clock and calendar in view so you can give it a place in your time track. If it's money, count it, feel it, deposit it—in your mind's eye.

You may seek greater maturity of mind in that private universe of yours. Then give yourself the H-C instructions that:

- You will know and live what is good.

- You will understand and reveal in yourself true humility.

- You will see the best in every person, regardless of

wealth, nation, culture, age, race, sex, or religion.

But you have to reach for it.

Man's mind is like a giant laser. Properly focused, and with the full power turned on with H-C, it can reach anywhere, produce anything.

Can you see clearly what you want?

Then do so. With this desire in your mind's eye, power your mind by having a strong conviction that you are getting what you desire.

Men who have learned this secret have become millionaires.

People use this power everyday. They attract anything from lost dogs to lovers, from needed information to transportation, from a dime to make a phone call to financial security for life.

And everything that exists in our civilized world started with a focused, powered image. The building you are in now, your kitchen range, even the chair you are sitting in, and the book you are holding in your hand—all started with an image in a mind.

Do you want a more responsible job?

See yourself in it.

Do you want to get out of debt?

See yourself free and clear.

Do you want to travel anywhere in the world?

See yourself en route.

Do you want to love and be loved?

See it happening.

Do you want a bigger and better home?

See yourself living in it.

Do you want to do your job better?

See yourself as a wiz at it.

Do you want success? What kind of success?

See yourself successful in any way you want. You are be-coming successful.

Get into your relaxed position, either with your instant H-C command or a finger levitation. See your life as you want it to be.

Do it now.

It will be.